OPEN FOR CHILDREN

**For Those Interested in
Early Childhood Education**

OPEN FOR CHILDREN

For Those Interested in Early Childhood Education

Judith Danoff

Director of Child Care/Early Childhood Education
Kingsborough Community College

Vicki Breitbart

Adjunct, Child Care/Early Childhood Education
Kingsborough Community College

Elinor Barr

Assistant Professor, Child Care/Early Childhood Education
Kingsborough Community College

McGraw-Hill Book Company

New York St. Louis San Francisco Auckland Bogotá Düsseldorf Johannesburg
London Madrid Mexico Montreal New Delhi Panama Paris São Paulo
Singapore Sydney Tokyo Toronto

OPEN FOR CHILDREN

**For Those Interested in
Early Childhood Education**

2 3 4 5 6 7 8 9 D O D O 7 8 3 2 1 0 9 8

This book was set in Primer by Black Dot, Inc. The editors were Stephen D. Dragin and Susan Gamer; the designer was Jo Jones; the production supervisor was Angela Kardovich. The drawings were done by J & R Services, Inc.
The cover photographs and the photograph on page 21 were taken by Mary Danoff; all other photographs were taken by Eric Breitbart.
R. R. Donnelley & Sons Company was printer and binder.

Library of Congress Cataloging in Publication Data

Danoff, Judith.
  Open for children.

  Includes bibliographies and index.
  1. Education, Preschool. I. Breitbart,
Vicki, joint author. II. Barr, Elinor, joint
author. III. Title.
LB1140.2.D36   372.21   76-26669
ISBN 0-07-015343-4
ISBN 0-07-015342-6 pbk.

*This book is dedicated to
Kimmer Danoff and Joshua Breitbart,
both in their first weeks of life,
and to all the people in their world,
in the hope that it will help them have
fulfilling experiences in early childhood.*

CONTENTS

Foreword   ix

Preface   xi

1 THE STUDENT TEACHER   1

Teaching in Society   2

Looking Forward to a New Experience   4

Attitudes with Children   6

The Teacher's Role   7

Interpersonal Relationships   11

Your Evaluation   16

Further Readings   17

2 THE CHILD   19

Learning Is a Process   20

The Whole Child   22

Understanding the Whole Child   25

The Development of Children's Thinking   31

Observing the Whole Child   34

Further Readings   40

3 THE CHILD IN SCHOOL   41

Meeting the School   42

Separation: The Adjustment to the First School Experience   43

Parents in School   48

Discipline and Self-Control   50

Further Readings   57

4 THE CLASSROOM   59

Room Arrangement   60

Evaluating the Effectiveness of a Learning Environment   71

Room-Arrangement Kit   74

Further Readings   76

5 LEARNING IN THE CLASSROOM   77

How the Child Learns about Things   78

Further Activities for Matching, Sorting, and Grouping   82

Learning through Dramatic Play   85

The Value of Play in Cognitive Learning   88

Further Readings   92

6 THE CURRICULUM   93

The Integrated Curriculum   94

Language Arts   97

Mathematics   117

Science: An Attitude and a Method   130

Social Studies   138

Music   145

Art   152

Health and Physical Education   164

Outdoor Play   169

Further Readings   176

7 EXPANDING THE CURRICULUM   179

The Integrated Curriculum in Action   180

Blocks   180

Trips for Young Children   183

Woodworking   188

Cooking   194

Further Readings   208

Glossary   210

Appendix   213

Index   221

FOREWORD

For the person who wants to teach young children, *Open for Children* provides a good introduction. For those who are also open to their growth, it will be the first of many experiences involved in the making of a competent teacher. It starts, quite appropriately, with the student teacher, a person with intelligence and feelings. The problems the authors pose as early as the first chapter reveal their belief that teaching requires reflection on one's own behavior as well as on the behavior of children.

The children are introduced next, with special focus on the years from three to five. The discussion is not limited to those years, however. It provides some sense of where the three-year-old has been developmentally, as well as where the five-year-old is heading. At the same time there is allowance for the individuality that characterizes each child. Here the student begins to learn that most basic skill of the early childhood teacher—observation. Next, he or she confronts the child in school. The emphasis is on the network of feelings and relationships the teacher needs to understand in order to be effective. Following that comes the physical arrangement of the classroom, something that can either enhance or impede children's learning.

The sections on curriculum provide many possibilities. The student need never be at a loss for things to do with the children. Furthermore, the authors show how the activities for young children extend into the more traditional subject-oriented curriculum, and how in turn these subjects may form an integrated whole. It is well that the emphasis is on children's action and play, for despite much experimentation with different curriculum models, we do not know that any one model is inherently superior to any other. We do know, as the authors imply, that preschool children do not necessarily organize their thoughts as the adults who plan the curriculum expect them to.

It takes time for the teacher to come to terms with the children's thinking and to learn to pace each child's interests with appropriate new experiences. This may be a matter of skillful questioning, always at the level of the child's understanding; or it may involve watchful waiting as the child deals, emotionally as well as intellectually, with some aspect of his or her environment.

This book opens to the prospective teacher the richness and complexity of early childhood education. In the space of a few pages it provides a comprehensive picture of what the teacher does and the basic skills he or she needs. This, as the student teacher will eventually realize, is only a beginning.

The competent teacher draws on an ever-increasing knowledge of the many factors, both individual and cultural, that are involved in children's development and learning. Respect of and understanding for children's parents grows apace. Views of curriculum become more differentiated; and the reasons for choosing one approach and not another are better understood and articulated.

Today's changing world demands that teachers be flexible enough to meet new situations, without losing sight of either the short-term or the long-term consequences for children.

Millie Almy
Professor of Education
University of California, Berkeley

PREFACE

We believe that good schools and day-care centers with competent, knowledgeable, and caring teachers will help children to become adults who will contribute to a productive and humane society. Yet education of high quality is becoming harder to achieve every day.

We are preparing this book at a time when the government is making drastic cutbacks in funding for our schools. All human services are under attack. The crisis in our economy has exposed certain distortions of priorities in society. Certain industries continue to prosper while budgets are balanced at the expense of basic human needs.

We write this book with hope for the future. We believe that people will see the importance of good schools and day-care centers and will work, locally and nationally, to change the present situation. It will be necessary to break down the prejudices that have divided people. It will take the dedicated and continuous efforts of large numbers of people to achieve our goal.

We ask our readers to understand that people involved in teaching have a commitment to those they serve. To meet this commitment, they must work in the classroom, and in the society as a whole, to maintain and improve our human services. 1977

ACKNOWLEDGMENTS

This book results from our teaching experiences. We wish to thank all the children and parents we have known, and all the students who have helped us understand what student teachers want and need to learn. They have been an important source of our learning.

In Chapter 4, the section headed "Evaluating the Effectiveness of the Learning Environment" is based on the work of Harriet K. Cuffaro; and the section headed "Room Arrangement" is based on material from V. Breitbart, *The Day Care Book*, Knopf, New York 1974, copyright V. Breitbart.

In Chapter 6, the section headed "Reading Skills" is based on an article by Judith Danoff and Felicia Gross; and the section headed "Children's Art: The Creative Process" was previously published by Judith Danoff in *Children Today* (H.E.W.), July–August 1975.

We thank the Flatbush Action Community Day Care Center (Magic Years) and the Young Men and Young Women's Hebrew Association of East Flatbush for allowing us to photograph their children, staff, and classrooms. We are grateful to the Bank Street School for Children for some of the photographs in the section "Room Arrangement." The photograph on page 21 was taken by Mary Danoff. All other photographs in this book are by Eric Breitbart.

We also wish to thank Diane Rubin, who worked in the Early Childhood Education program at Kingsborough Community College. Her assistance in the preparation of this book helped make it possible.

We acknowledge the support and encouragement given to us and our program by President Leon Goldstein and Dean Michael Zibrin of Kingsborough Community College, and the support of the Bureau of Two Year College Program, New York State Education Department, which provided invaluable resources in the initial stages of development.

Finally, we thank Mary Danoff for her creative assistance on our manuscript.

Judith Danoff

Vicki Breitbart

Elinor Barr

1 THE STUDENT TEACHER

TEACHING IN SOCIETY

Students entering the teaching profession have to critically ask themselves, "Why do I really want to be a teacher?" Perhaps you feel that children represent all that is "good and true" in a society that has lost touch with the old virtues of goodness and truth. You might feel it would be a refreshing change to be with people who are honest, who never deceive, and who always tell you how they think and feel. How valid is your impression of children's honesty? A child may say "I hate you" and really mean "I need more attention from you." He is being honest, but we need to interpret his words to get to his true meaning. A mother may tell you that her oldest child loves the new baby "so much that he has to be watched." He hugs the baby so tightly that she cries. The older child knows he is hurting the baby, but he has found a socially accepted way to express his real feelings. Sometimes a child says that everything is fine, but careful observation tells you another story. His face is tense, his fingers fidget at his pockets, and his foot begins to twist. You can see from his nonverbal behavior that he is not putting his real feelings into words.

Some students enter the profession because they want to "be loved" and to "give love." You needn't feel guilty about these reasons. Personal satisfaction is an important aspect of a wise career choice. However, "love" is a term that must be carefully examined. In our culture, physical beauty is something we are constantly conditioned to admire, seek, or attain. Do you "love" children because they are physically attractive—because they are "cute" or "adorable"? Perhaps you do feel this way, to some degree, but when you begin to spend time with children in a classroom situation, you will quickly learn that they are not objects to be admired or cuddled. They are young people with very definite personalities and with needs that must be defined and met by their teachers if they are to grow and develop. Do you "love" children because they are little and helpless and because this makes it easy for you to satisfy your own needs to be protective—to feel strong and in control of their lives? As students of early childhood education, you will soon understand that young children grow and develop best in an atmosphere that allows them to discover their own strengths and abilities, and you will learn that overprotectiveness is inhibiting to growth.

The important issue related to all these questions is your honest examination of what your feelings really mean and of the way these feelings might affect your work with children. You can use this insight to help you clarify your individual relationships with children and to enable you to provide experiences for them that allow for healthy growth.

Some students enter the teaching profession because they feel sorry for poor children and want to help them. It is important for us to recognize that all children need help in a learning situation. The role of the teacher, with all children, is to enable them to feel competent, to gain skills, and to see themselves as effective human beings. The teacher

Each child approaches the student teacher differently, and the student teacher can meet the individual needs of several children in one activity.

needs empathy and understanding for all the children she teaches. This means she needs to acquaint herself with the economic, social, and cultural conditions of the lives of her students.

For those student teachers who have grown up without economic need, teaching in an economically impoverished community is a new and often frightening experience. How do you feel about this community, where people have a different life style from your own? How do you feel about the children in this community, whose everyday experiences are different from yours? These are important questions for each student teacher to face with total honesty. Do you look at the poor with pity and fear, or do you try to understand the reasons, within the society, for the conditions in which they live?

Some student teachers who have been economically deprived find that they resent children they encounter who are financially more advantaged than they are. It is important to be aware of these feelings. Again it is vital to stress the value of self-examination. Knowing who you are, in relation to the people you are going to work with and the children you are going to teach, will help you to be a more effective teacher and human being.

Equally important is the need to be aware of others. Teachers need to learn about the society in which they live.

Teachers need to respect the many cultures that exist in our society. They must understand the history, culture, and political and economic necessities of the many groups within the structure of society if they want to understand their strengths and problems. Teachers who have this understanding are seen by parents as people who are really interested in the welfare of their children. This makes it possible for parents and teachers to form a healthy alliance.

Education students often ask, "Why do I have to waste my time in economics and history courses?" Such courses are not a waste of time. An understanding of the forces of society, past and present, is imperative for the fulfillment of the teacher's role and the achievement of his or her goal.

Sometimes as education students become more and more involved in the world of teaching, they begin to disassociate themselves from other aspects of the society. You must recognize that our schools developed in the way they did because of society's needs. What goes on in society has a direct impact on our lives and on our schools. As a teacher, as a human being, you will be affected by everything that happens around you all your life. Government changes, wars, depression, the ecology, nutrition, the distribution of goods and services—all will affect you directly.

LOOKING FORWARD TO A NEW EXPERIENCE

As someone about to begin student teaching, you are now looking forward to many new experiences this semester. In your early childhood classes you will visit different schools, work in a classroom, meet many new people, and use some unfamiliar materials. You will also be introduced to new ideas and concepts.

Like all new experiences, this one may create mixed feelings:

You're excited about working with children.
You're excited about how much there is to learn.
You're excited about becoming a teacher.

At the same time:

You're not sure what will be expected of you.

You're not sure you will be able to do what is expected.
You're afraid the children might not like you.

From your own experiences in school you know the lasting impact teachers can have. They affect not only what you learn but also your ability to learn, your love of learning, and your image of yourself. You recognize that teaching is creative and meaningful work but that it requires a great deal of know-how and commitment. This gives you a sense of importance about the work you are doing. It may make you want to get the most out of the experience. It may also make you feel uncomfortable and fearful.

Being anxious about this new experience, you may find yourself doing some of the following things.

You may look for faults in others. Do you remember your first day in a new school? Perhaps you decided that no one there was really worth bothering with, rather than admit you were frightened that no one would want to be *your* friend.

You may be overly critical of things around you. If you've ever been away at camp, you may remember everyone complaining about the food. It was certainly easier than confronting your feelings of homesickness.

You may withdraw from the situation or become absorbed in busywork. Have you ever been to a party where you hardly knew anyone and found yourself frozen in a corner, eating potato chips like mad.

These are all ways of being defensive. It will be easier if you can just relax and accept your anxious feelings. Remember that as a teacher you will need to help children deal with complex feelings. You will have to help them face a lot of changes and make adjustments to new situations. The better you know your own feelings, the more you will bring to your work.

The following points may be helpful to you.

Your feelings are common reactions to new experiences. All new experiences imply some challenge or some change. It's natural to resist change until you become familiar with the new approaches and new skills that are required. You will feel uncomfortable until you are confident that you can succeed.

You can't expect to know, now, what will take a long time to learn. You are in school precisely because you are not expected to know how to teach yet; for this you need the training you are in the process of getting.

There is no "perfect teacher." The most effective teaching is part of a process of caring, trying, observing, evaluating—and trying again. You are at the beginning of this process, but there is really no end to the kind of questioning and constant growth it takes to work well with children.

There is no one way of doing things. There are basic guidelines about working effectively with children—these will be presented and discussed in your courses—but there is a lot of room for your own personal interpretations.

Children aren't seriously affected by isolated mistakes. A single period of time each week is a small piece of a much larger picture. Children are exposed to many different adults and a variety of experiences; growing up is a very complex experience. A "mistake" in a relationship between a student and a child often provides an opportunity for them both to grow.

Children are generally accepting of people. When children say things like "Go away" or "I don't like you," usually they are expressing the way they feel at the moment. They do not really mean such statements to be "forever." Sometimes comments like these are a child's way of finding out who you are and how you react to negative interaction.

You will have a chance to try out a number of things outside the field-placement classroom. You will use many new materials in your curriculum courses before you will have to use them in a class with children. You will also have the opportunity to discuss your field experiences in your early childhood course.

You will be working with an adviser who will encourage you and support what you do. Advisers are people who have had experiences similar to the ones you are going through. They expect mistakes to be made and can anticipate some of them. They can help you analyze the causes of behavior and in this way provide you with experiences that foster your growth as a teacher. Their role is to help you gain information, master skills, and increase your sensitivity. They are there to help you develop self-awareness and to understand how your own experiences are helping or hindering your work. Your adviser will try to help you understand the ideas presented in your other courses and apply these ideas in the classroom setting. He or she is committed to working with you to help you find your own unique style of teaching.

ATTITUDES WITH CHILDREN

Think of adults whom you have liked—teachers, supervisors, or group leaders, for example. One reason you probably liked them was because they liked you. You felt this.

You felt it when they helped you.
You felt it when they appreciated something you did.
You felt it when they showed you how to do it better.
You felt it when they prevented you from losing control.
You felt it when they understood how you felt and accepted your feelings.

These people didn't necessarily excel in things, but they did help you to improve in some way. They weren't like friends of your own age—they remained adults to you, adults who cared about you.

Did they have a great need to beat you in games? Probably not. Were they inordinate show-offs? We doubt it.

Did they push you around and constantly bark orders at you? No.

Did they seem to ignore you by letting you do whatever you wanted to do? No.

Did they say, "Don't be a crybaby"? That certainly wouldn't have helped. If you were crying, they probably recognized your pain, comforted you, and said something that helped: "I know that hurts." "Let's see what we can do to make you feel better."

Try to remember such people as you work with groups. This is not the time to assert yourself and show your abilities and skills. *You are strong if you can use your skills to make your group feel their strengths and skills.*

You may not be a great baseball player, but you can show a child how to hold a bat. You may be a marvelous baseball player. You don't have to prove it. You can still show a child how to hold a bat.

You must have confidence in people's ability to do and learn. Your confidence will help build their self-confidence and will give them faith in you. The more confident you are, the better you can perform. The more confident you are, the more you can enjoy what you are doing.

Your attitude with a group and your attitude with the individuals in the group will set the tone for your successful use of the skills you possess.

THE TEACHER'S ROLE

As a future teacher, respect and trust children's eagerness to learn. No one can give knowledge. As a teacher, you can create a learning climate. You can create an environment that exposes learners to exciting choices. The learner must choose to learn and must be ready and able to learn.

See yourself as the facilitator of the discovery. You supply and structure the materials. As children discover, you pose the questions that bring their discovery to the conscious level. As children discuss their experiences, they integrate the learning. This means that you must always be aware of the discoveries. You must help equip children so that they can express their own ideas in their own words. You will not "do" for children; you will do all you can to help them "do" for themselves.

Even though you may be a student in the classroom, the child will see you as a teacher. It is therefore important for you to understand what your attitudes are and to recognize that they affect the children with

The teacher is part of children's social interaction but does not direct it.

whom you are working. Your values and attitudes are communicated to children in many verbal and nonverbal ways every day. The way you talk to children, what you say to them, how you feel about them, and the way you act—all affect children and the way they will behave. You should remember that:

You can't treat children insensitively and then expect them to become confident and trusting adults.

You can't order children about and then expect them to develop a sense of competence in solving problems and confronting challenges.

You can't be overly critical of children and then expect them to have a strong self-image.

It is also true that:

If you enjoy what you are doing, children will sense this and will be more likely to enjoy what they are doing.

If you are sensitive, children are more likely to be this way.

If you treat children with compassion and respect, they are more likely to act this way.

In order to create the atmosphere of confidence, trust, and mutual respect that is necessary for the full development of each child, teachers *do not*:

Dominate the program
Continually exert their authority and make children feel powerless
Foster competition that pits one child against another and limits learning and growth
Pressure children and continually express disappointment
Humiliate children with sarcastic or negative remarks
Talk about children in front of them or laugh at their efforts.

Teachers *do* the following:

They give children a sense of security and belonging. Children need to feel safe. They need to know that the teacher is someone who is concerned about their health and well-being, who listens when they talk, who laughs with them and talks in ways they can understand, who supports and encourages them when they need it, and who sets reasonable limits to protect them when necessary, without ever making them feel stupid, ugly, bad, or inadequate.

They make children feel that their work is respected. It is important for the teacher to protect children's concentration on their work as well as the work itself. A child can get awfully discouraged if her block building is continually knocked down or if her painting winds up in the garbage.

They plan activities that foster independence and success. The kind of success we are talking about here is not the kind that rests on competition with others or is measured by tests. It is the kind that involves individual growth—the kind which develops a person's feelings of confidence in mastering skills and working with others and which fosters in him a feeling of well-being about who he is and what he does.

They demonstrate an understanding of child development by providing appropriate activities and materials. Materials in the classroom should be varied and interesting, as well as appropriate for the needs and capacities of children at each stage of growth. Activities should provide opportunities for choice and experimentation, with an emphasis on the child's growth and not on teacher satisfaction.

They treat each child as a unique individual. The teacher recognizes each child's special way of expressing himself. The teacher understands that a child's behavior is not arbitrary; it always reflects how the child feels and who the child is. A teacher observes children carefully and looks for clues as to how to guide each child in that child's own way.

They help children handle conflicts. A teacher does not solve problems for children but presents alternatives so that children can solve problems for themselves. In conflicts between children, the teacher encourages the children to work it out by themselves. The teacher helps them to talk about the conflict, to understand what started it, and to decide what solution would be fair to everyone involved.

They accept children's feelings. A teacher knows that when a child hurts himself, it really hurts; when a child is angry, he has a right to be angry. The teacher accepts and respects the child's feelings while helping the child to find socially acceptable ways to handle them.

They guide children's learning. The teacher knows each child's abilities, strengths, and weaknesses in all areas of development. The teacher observes and stands ready to offer new learning opportunities with familiar tasks, to present new and challenging experiences which will provide additional successes, and to present satisfying ways of relating to others.

They act as role models. What the teacher says and does must be consistent. For example, if two teachers in a classroom want the children to work cooperatively with one another, they must work together as a team themselves, showing respect for each other's individual contributions.

They show respect for other adults who are important to the child. The way young children feel about themselves is closely linked to their feelings about family, friends, and community. Teachers who recognize and respect this will be more effective in the classroom. If teachers and parents show one another's concern for feelings and try to mobilize their collective strength to build the best possible program for the children, the children will be encouraged to be cooperative, sensitive, inventive, and responsible people too.

Some Typical Problem Situations Teachers Face

Marilyn is a four-year-old who is working in the block corner. She has built a totally enclosed structure (no openings on the sides or top). Inside, she has put a small fire truck and an assortment of animals. She tells you it's a firehouse. What might you ask, say, or do to help Marilyn clarify her ideas and expand her information and understanding?

Jane and Peter are teachers in a classroom. At lunchtime, Jane tells Peter to serve one of the children, Sarah, a spoonful of string beans and then make her eat all of them. Sarah says she hates string beans and won't eat them. If you were Peter, what would you do if you didn't want to force Sarah to eat but wanted to maintain a good working relationship with your co-worker?

You are Jennifer's teacher. You have saved her paintings, and you give them to her to take home. When her mother calls for her and sees the paintings, she says, "I don't want any more of these things at home," and throws them in the trash. Jennifer's eyes start to water, and she seems upset. What would you do if you wanted to show your concern for Jennifer without interfering in the relationship between mother and child?

Sally and Pat are teachers. Sally has just yelled at a child, William, who has spilled paint on the floor. As she approaches William, he runs away. Sally asks Pat to catch him. Pat feels she wouldn't have yelled at William and doesn't think running after children is an appropriate or effective response. If you were Pat, what would you do if you wanted to maintain a good working relationship with Sally while supporting William in this conflict?

For several days, John, a four-year-old in your group, has been watching other children climbing the jungle gym. Today you are standing near him when the other children again take off for the top. What would you do if you felt John wanted to join the others but was afraid he might fall?

Rachel is a three-year-old. She has just walloped another child in your class. Your co-worker, Susan, has just grabbed Rachel and hit her. You disagree with your co-worker's handling of the situation. What would you do (1) if you had seen the incident that led up to Rachel's hitting and (2) if you hadn't seen anything but Rachel hitting and being hit?

INTERPERSONAL RELATIONSHIPS

Your student teaching experience will be a unique opportunity to use your newly acquired skills and your knowledge of early childhood. It will also give you a chance to experience the reality of the classroom, with its variety of human relationships. Your competencies in, and understanding of, early childhood education will directly affect the quality of the relationships you establish. These relationships will in turn affect what you learn in the field placement and what you can offer to the class.

Each of you will work in different settings, and the structure of the schools will vary depending on their organization and philosophy. You will probably come into contact with the following people.

The Supervisor

This is usually the first person to greet you. The supervisor will tell you about the school's administrative structure, regulations, educational philosophy, and dress code. In some schools the supervisor is the

The teacher is supporting the child's special discovery.

principal; in other schools he or she is the director. The supervisor usually has had a good deal of training and experience in education, educational supervision, or both. While the supervisor is responsible for the entire school, the two of you will most likely have little contact after this initial meeting.

The Teacher

The classroom teacher is usually certified and has had prior classroom experience. He or she is accountable to the supervisor and the parents and is responsible for the program and for all the children, staff members, volunteers, and student teachers in the room.

The Assistant Teacher or Paraprofessional

The assistant teacher or paraprofessional works directly with children but usually does not have the same academic training as the teacher and therefore receives a much lower salary. The assistant teacher works closely with the teacher in planning, making preparations, and conducting activities in the classroom and often performs at such a high level that the observer cannot always tell which is the teacher and which is the assistant. Many paraprofessionals, particularly those who have worked in the classroom for several years, have excellent skills and sensitivity to children's needs. External circumstances, however, have not allowed many skilled paraprofessionals to achieve the necessary academic training. This may cause conflict between the paraprofessional and the student teacher, who upon graduation will be eligible to receive a higher salary. The student teacher must be sensitive to this possibility.

Parents

Student teachers and assistant teachers are sometimes asked to avoid all discussions with parents about children's behavior. This can be uncomfortable when a parent comes to call for a child and directly asks the student teacher, "How was Johnny today?" The student teacher need not be at a loss for a response. It is possible to give a direct answer that deals with the child's activity, presents a fact, and doesn't imply any judgment—"He made a painting today" or "He was busy building with blocks," for example.

Your Role in the Classroom

Schools receive student teachers as part of a professional obligation to help train new professionals. Most teachers will welcome your presence

The student teacher interacts with some of the children while the teacher is busy elsewhere—this helps enrich learning for the entire group.

in the classroom and try to make you feel comfortable. It is generally agreed that student teachers do best if they are allowed to interact with the children as soon as possible, but teachers have different ways of working with student teachers. One might say, "You may sit and observe for an hour." Another might say, "You may sit and observe or move around and talk to the children, whichever is more comfortable for you." Still another might tell you to go immediately to a particular group and conduct a certain activity.

You may prefer one approach to another. However, it is best to follow the teacher's initial direction. The relationship between you and the teacher is just beginning, and the teacher will feel more comfortable in giving you some responsibility if she sees that you are cooperative.

Sometimes you may find that you are asked to observe and are never told to interact. This can create a frustrating situation for you, and a discussion with your college supervisor will be necessary. In many of these situations the classroom teacher may tell the supervisor, "The student teacher has never once interacted with the children or helped with the materials." At these times a three-way conference between you, the teacher, and the supervisor can be helpful in clarifying your role and the expectations of the classroom teacher.

Your primary reason for being in the field is to develop your understanding of child development and your teaching skills. You are not expected to do work that is not related to your educational growth. Yet doing some clerical work and some clean-up is definitely part of the teaching role. Doing nothing *but* clerical work and clean-up, however, is a misuse of your time and should be discussed with your college supervisor.

Your Relationship to Others in the Classroom

Your initial reaction to the classroom teacher may be very extreme. The situation is complicated by the biases and stereotypes each of us may have about the teaching role. You may find yourself saying, "All teachers are bad. They are against children. I will save these children and protect them from the teacher. I will do the opposite of what she does. What she does is all wrong."

Or you may say, "All teachers are wonderful, superior people. They know everything worth knowing. I will copy the words, phrases, voice quality, and gestures of this teacher. Then I too will be marvelous."

Neither reaction can be correct. Teachers are human, and as human beings they will have various ways of reacting to situations and people. Their actions will be motivated by a very complex set of ideas and feelings. The purpose of the field placement is not to have you judge or idolize the teacher with whom you are working. Rather, it is to give you some insight into different styles of teaching and into the learning process. In the end, of course, you will find your own individual style.

Any questions, concerns, and problems that may come up regarding the classroom situation can be discussed with the college supervisor. You are a guest in the school and are expected to follow the school regulations and the teacher's directions. It is the college supervisor's responsibility to help you resolve any problems you may encounter in the field.

It is hoped that you will find yourself in a situation where the teacher sees all the adults in the room as part of a team, working in the best interests of the children. In this situation the teacher will be happy when she finds that members of the team can establish relationships with some individual children she can't reach. She will be delighted if a child has found someone to help him grow, someone to meet his needs. A teacher who is interested in the growth and development of all the children in her class will not be threatened by these relationships. She will reinforce the development of these positive relationships by scheduling team meetings to discuss the educational goals she has for individual children, and she will support the work of each team member.

There is no doubt that you will learn best in a climate that allows for the full development of each individual. But what do you do if you find yourself in a placement where the teacher has a completely different philosophical approach? In these situations, it is best to remember that it *is* the *teacher's* class. Your first responsibility is to discuss your concerns with your college supervisor. He or she may be able to arrange a time for you to work with a small group of children, in your own way. The supervisor may come and act as your assistant during this time. Several successful experiences like these may give the teacher some new ideas and give you the support you need to feel that you are a competent student teacher.

Perhaps your supervisor will suggest that you discuss with the teacher the discrepancies you find between the teacher's philosophy and your own understanding of a given situation. Such discussions sometimes result in a teacher's accepting the different point of view or in the student teacher's understanding the teacher's action.

You might explain to the teacher that you had learned it was best to let children decide where to write their names on their paintings. The teacher could say, "What a good idea! I never thought of that." Or the teacher might say, "I want it on the back of the painting so that it doesn't interfere with the child's design." This interaction has given you a chance to understand the reasons for the teacher's position and can give you more to go on in the future when you make decisions for your own classroom.

It is important to remember that children are upset and confused when two adults in the room have opposing points of view. In this situation, if they are not able to get what they want from one adult, they will try to relate to the other one. This is not in anyone's interest. It is not necessary to withdraw or cover up your point of view, but it is important to discuss conflicting opinions *after* the session is over.

YOUR EVALUATION

Working in a classroom is a challenging experience. Not only are you trying out curriculum ideas, but you are also learning the equally important techniques of working with others. Like all situations involving a variety of human interactions, it is difficult and often confusing. To further complicate this process, you are also being observed by many people. Teachers, other staff members, parents, and your college supervisor—all see you in action. This may be difficult for you. It should be comforting to know that it does get easier with time and experience and that the trained staff around you expect you to make some mistakes. These people will not use such incidents to undermine your work but will discuss them with you in order to help you learn.

All aspects of your work will be evaluated. Some concerns will be your ability to:

Accept and apply supervision and direction
Relate to, and work well with, adults
Interact with children and facilitate their learning
Apply theory to practice
Cope with a variety of situations

The criticism and help you will be offered will, it is hoped, give you a better understanding of your strengths and weaknesses in coping with this new experience. It is through this understanding that you can develop the teaching style that is most effective for you.

FURTHER READINGS

Almy, M.: *The Early Childhood Educator at Work*, McGraw-Hill, New York, 1975.

Ashton-Warner, Sylvia: *Teacher*, Simon & Shuster, New York, 1963.

Cook, A., and H. Mack: *The Teacher's Role*, Macmillan, London, 1971.

Jersild, A.: *When Teachers Face Themselves*, Columbia University, Bureau of Publications, New York, 1955.

Klopf, G., G. Bowman, and Joy Adena: *A Learning Team: Teacher and Auxiliary*, Bank Street College of Education, New York, 1969.

Moustakas, C.: *The Authentic Teacher*, rev. ed., Howard A. Doyle, Cambridge, Mass., 1966.

Otty, N.: *Learner Teacher*, Harmondsworth, Middlesex, England, 1972.

2 THE CHILD

LEARNING IS A PROCESS

As a teacher, you will be equally responsible for both the learning and the growth of every child with whom you work. You will need to know a great deal about child development in order to fulfill this responsibility. You will need to understand how children grow, what outside forces affect them, and what their needs are at different stages of development. Having this information can provide you with some guidelines, but you will still have to find that something special about each child you meet.

In your work you will learn that in some ways children are alike—all the children in your group may be of a similar age and come from the same neighborhood—and that you can make some general statements about them. Yet their similarities should never mask the range of experiences and the variety of personalities in any group. They should never overshadow the unique combination of strengths and weaknesses of each individual child. Take a look at an individual child. What do you see? The hair color and style, the skin color, the clothes—but this doesn't really tell you about *this* child.

As a teacher, you will have the challenge of maintaining expectations for all children while helping each child in his or her own terms. In order to be an effective teacher, you will need to know not only how each child is like others but also, more importantly, how each child is like no other. General statements about *all* children should be made only in order to help us understand *each* child. Taking a look at one child can help us understand all children. Clyde Kluckhohn says, "In some ways—all men are like all other men. In some ways—some men are like some other men. In some ways—no man is like another man." *

Sarah is four years old. When she came to the prekindergarten class for the first time, she had already learned a lot. She walked with firm, sure steps; she could run without "toddling"; she could talk in sentences that were for the most part clear and understandable to adults; and she could perform many self-help tasks, like putting on her coat and feeding herself.

In the classroom it was also clear that Sarah was confident enough to try new things, to reach out to others, to make her needs known, to take risks, and even to make mistakes.

No one taught Sarah these things. No one sat her down and drilled her in any of these skills. But she was allowed to explore the world around her; she used all her senses—she tasted, saw, heard, touched, and smelled an exciting variety of things that were provided for her. Her body matured, she got a chance to move around, and she gradually gained greater control over her arms and legs—and indeed over all her responses.

Sarah was also surrounded by people who talked to her, held her, and

---

*George F. Kneller, *Introduction to the Philosophy of Education*, Wiley, New York, 1971. p. 46

Free exploration is the foundation of a child's learning and growth.

cared for her. They had realistic expectations for Sarah. They encouraged her to do what she was capable of doing. She wasn't pushed to run before she could walk; she wasn't made to write while she still enjoyed scribbling. People didn't rush Sarah or demand immediate results that would have meant a loss of confidence. Instead, Sarah was allowed to fully enjoy each stage of her development, she was guided to every new step, and she was praised for her efforts and accomplishments.

Now Sarah is an active, curious, and content child. She has learned a lot, and—what is just as important—she is eager to learn more and is confident that she *will*!

While Sarah is a unique person, her example helps us see that:

Learning takes place from birth.

Children learn as total human beings.

Each aspect of development is related to all others—feeling confident and secure affects the development of different skills.

Children learn from everything around them.

Children need a variety of real experiences.

It is important to understand and respect the natural sequence of children's learning and growth.

THE WHOLE CHILD

Children's learning and growth involve Physical, Emotional, Social and Intellectual development.

Physical development This refers to children's bodies and their motor development, to their senses (hearing, sight, touch, taste, and smell), and to their physical abilities and disabilities.

Emotional development This refers to children's feelings and reactions, (comfort or discomfort, pleasure or pain, etc.) and to their needs (such as the need for protection and independence) and how they are met.

Social development This refers to children's interactions with other people, including their culture and their community and the sex and work roles in the society.

Intellectual development This refers to children's thinking, including observing and perceiving, receiving and processing information, problem solving, and communicating (listening and speaking).

All Areas of Development Are Interrelated

Every experience affects many, if not all, aspects of development simultaneously. For instance, when a baby is hungry, cries, and is given a bottle, the child is:

Physically experiencing sensations in the stomach

Emotionally experiencing discomfort and then a relief of this discomfort

Socially experiencing the relief of this discomfort by another person

Intellectually experiencing crying as a form of communicating and getting a reaction.

Water play allows for social interaction, intellectual learning, eye-hand coordination, motor coordination, and emotional satisfaction.

In an early childhood classroom, when the children are playing with water, they:

Physically can be developing the muscle coordination involved in pouring. They can also be experiencing the sensations of wet and of warm or cold.

Emotionally can be experiencing the feeling of the water flowing over their hands as soothing and enjoyable.

Socially can be sharing the water and the materials with other children.

Intellectually can be observing such things as the flowing of the water, the capacity of each container, the objects that sink or float, and the weight of a full container compared with the weight of an empty one.

Each aspect of development affects all the others. Physical, emotional, social, and intellectual development are all interrelated. How children feel about themselves will affect their ability to learn. The abilities children develop will affect their self-image and sense of worth. Here is an example:

Emotionally Jane feels she is not capable and has a negative sense of herself.

Socially this causes her to avoid making friends or to have difficult relationships.

Physically she sits at home all day and watches television. This impairs her motor development.

Intellectually she is so absorbed with her problem that she is not able to learn all she can.

Emotionally this makes her feel less capable.

Growth and Development

The learning and growth of the child progress through successive stages. Each child is unique, and each has his or her own style of doing things, but the process of development is common to all. The actual length of time required for each stage may differ for different children, but the sequence of these stages is always the same. The list below shows the usual sequence.

THREE-YEAR-OLD	FIVE-YEAR-OLD
Physically: Walks well; can stand on one foot, but often looks off balance when running.	*Physically:* Is much more agile; has a good sense of balance.
Emotionally: Cries and hits as a form of expression	*Emotionally:* Can usually express feelings and settle disputes with language.
Socially: Has difficulty sharing.	*Socially:* Has adapted fairly well to group life. Is more interested in rules than a younger child.

THREE-YEAR-OLD	FIVE-YEAR-OLD
Intellectually: Uses sentences but has a relatively limited vocabulary; grammar is often confused.	*Intellectually:* Can express himself or herself in much greater detail; is more interested in recognizing printed words.

The development through the stages of growth is often uneven. Changes may occur rapidly in one stage and yet progress slowly through another. There will be bursts of energy and growth as well as periods of calm. At times, children will "gobble up" everything that is around them, and new abilities seem to blossom overnight. At other times, children will repeat the same task over and over and will want to surround themselves with familiar things and past loves. At these times, children seem to be "refueling." Sometimes children take one step back with every two steps forward. Just when they appear to be shifting to a new stage, they will revert back to earlier behavior.

Every child also develops different abilities at different rates of growth. For instance:

A child may have a five-year-old's ability to use language, while his or her physical abilities resemble those of a child of three.

A child who is able to build a complicated structure with blocks may become very upset if another child takes one of the blocks away.

A child who can read some simple words may become frantic when he can't remember where his mittens are.

Programs for the Whole Child

Any program that recognizes the interrelationship of all aspects of development takes a broad view of learning. It focuses on what is called the "whole child." It also maintains that while the process of development is the same for all children, the actual pattern of growth in each area is unique for each child.

UNDERSTANDING THE WHOLE CHILD

Planning for the individual child is based on an understanding of children in general. When teachers are familiar with the characteristics of children in a certain group, they can create an appropriate environment for learning and can set up the ongoing program. They are then free to provide for individual differences within this general framework.

CHILDREN FROM THREE TO FIVE

Characteristics	Needs	Suggestions for the Classroom Teacher
Physically: Are active and energetic.	Opportunities for play that involve their whole body.	Provide enough space for the children to move about freely. Provide running, jumping, and skipping activities. Provide climbing equipment.

Characteristics	Needs	Suggestions for the Classroom Teacher
Tire easily after periods of vigorous activity.	Balance between active and quiet play.	See that vigorous physical activity is followed by a story, a discussion, or a snack.
Are susceptible to many common childhood diseases.	Nutritious food. Good health care, including immunizations and checkups.	When meals are provided, see that they are well balanced. Provide snacks that include things like fruits and vegetables. Make informal ongoing checks on each child to determine his or her physical condition.
Are developing the ability to care for themselves.	Opportunities to develop independence.	Provide self-care tasks. Allow enough time for dressing. If necessary, start zippers for the children, but let them finish dressing themselves. Provide toys that help them practice things like lacing and buttoning. Let the children help prepare food; as much as possible, let them serve the food.
Are developing muscular control.	Opportunities to develop large-muscle coordination. Opportunities to develop fine-muscle coordination.	Provide games that include things like throwing and catching a ball and walking across a low beam. Provide pouring activities with water or sand. Provide toys like pegs and pegboards and scissors.
Exploring things around them; often are unable to determine what is dangerous.	A safe environment and adequate adult supervision.	Provide toys that, used properly, are safe for the children. Provide mats or a soft surface in climbing areas. When the children are using materials or are involved in activities that are potentially dangerous, provide clear directions and close supervision.
Emotional Can express a wide range of emotions— sometimes within a short period of time.	Recognition of feelings and fears.	Through stories and discussions, acknowledge a wide range of emotions, including sadness,

Characteristics	Needs	Suggestions for the Classroom Teacher
		happiness, anger, and love. Also, play games that include nonverbal expression, such as "Show someone you love him without saying a word," and "How do you look when something makes you sad?"
Are impulsive; usually respond quickly to situations.	A safe and secure atmosphere where they feel able to express emotions without hurting others or themselves.	When a child gets angry and hits another child, he or she should not be labeled "bad," but should be shown another way of expressing the anger and settling the dispute.
Are developing ways of channeling feelings, Often find it difficult to control emotions.	Opportunities to develop positive expressions of emotions.	Outdoor active play, woodworking, clay, and pounding boards are provided for general release of pent-up feelings.
Emotional state is affected by physical state. Can become irritable when hungry or tired.	Programs including snacks, meals if necessary, and ample time for rest.	An all-day program should include a time for rest after lunch.
Emotional state is affected by feeling of competence. Often feel powerless, unsure, and insecure. Can have many fears.	Opportunities to succeed. Opportunities to develop a sense of self-esteem, self-worth, belonging, and being loved. Opportunities to develop a sense of uniqueness.	Provide materials for a wide range of abilities. When a task is too difficult, help the children succeed by breaking it down into smaller, more manageable steps. For example, when a puzzle is too hard, have the child look at color or shape cues or take out only a few pieces at one time. Be sensitive to each child's needs. Praise each child's efforts. Comfort the children when necessary. Know each child's unique style of learning and his or her strengths and weaknesses. Take every opportunity to use each child's name and life experiences as part of the curriculum. Provide a chance for the children to use the same

Characteristics	Needs	Suggestions for the Classroom Teacher
		materials in different ways. For example, paper, glue, and a box of cut-up materials can be put together by each child in a unique way.

Social

Characteristics	Needs	Suggestions for the Classroom Teacher
Are basically egocentric: concerned primarily with themselves. Younger children may play near other children without really interacting. Gradually, a desire to be part of a group develops.	Opportunities to play alone as well as with other children. Encouragement, but not pressure to "join in."	Provide materials that the children can use alone but near other children—like a double easel—as well as group projects like murals.
The ability to accept group life—to cooperate, to take turns, to share—develops.	Opportunities to develop positive ways of interacting with others. Adults who act as role models, who are compassionate and cooperative, and who understand the child's difficulty in adapting to group life.	Provide group situations in which the children are encouraged but not forced to cooperate and share. Provide alternative ways of interacting. Help the children use language in social situations. Demonstrate positive ways of interacting by helping them when necessary, and by cooperating with co-workers.
Are developing independence but in many ways are still dependent on others.	Patient, caring, supportive adults who are able to give help without preventing the growth of independence. Opportunities to take responsibility.	Allow the children to do jobs that are necessary for the group. Provide a job chart. Give each child a turn caring for the animals, cleaning the tables, and giving out the snack. Help all the children take responsibility for cleaning up the room and putting away toys.
Are developing an understanding of their own roles and of adult roles.	Opportunities to try out a variety of roles they can see at home and in the community.	Provide dress-up clothes that stimulate dramatic play or roles such as those of parent, doctor, nurse, and firefighter.

Characteristics	Needs	Suggestions for the Classroom Teacher
Intellectual Are curious; learn best through active involvement, through their senses, and through direct experiences with things in the environment.	Opportunities to have sensory experiences—to see, touch, taste, smell and hear things around them. Opportunities to handle materials and make their own discoveries.	Provide firsthand experiences. For example, bring a guinea pig to the classroom and provide enough time and space for a small group of children to sit around and watch and handle the animal. Questions will most likely come from the children. For instance: "What is this?" "Where do guinea pigs come from?" The teacher is there to provide clear and simple explanations as well as to add her own questions when necessary.
Are concerned primarily with things that affect them personally.	Opportunities to investigate things that they see around them or experience in their everyday lives. Opportunities to see their names, their photographs, and their work as part of the classroom materials and displays.	Provide activities that enable the children to explore familiar materials like water, soap, and plastic containers. Classroom meetings may include discussions about the children's families and the work their parents do. Snacks can include many foods that the children also eat at home. The children can also make their own snacks—like French toast or pancakes—and can be encouraged to observe and discuss each step in the process. Books can be made about the children's experiences, including names of people they know.
Are concerned primarily with the present.	Opportunities to distinguish between reality and "make-believe."	Stories should be concerned with feelings and experiences that are familiar to the children.
Are increasing their attention span.	Opportunities to have a variety of experiences that are interesting to children.	For younger children, provide many different materials for similar learning experiences. Schedule group activities for relatively short periods

Characteristics	Needs	Suggestions for the Classroom Teacher
		of time. Provide games and toys which are open-ended (have more than one way of being played or played with) or which require a relatively short amount of time. Gradually introduce activities that require a longer attention span.
Are developing a sense of time.	Opportunities to recall experiences. Opportunities to plan and organize play.	At snack time the children can be asked what they did earlier in the morning. Classroom discussions on Monday morning should include what the children did over the weekend. The children should be asked to choose where they want to work each day—for example, a child might choose the block area. Block structures can be left intact and added to each day for as long as the children are interested.
Are developing the ability to "symbolize" experiences.	Opportunities to express ideas in a variety of ways. Opportunities to symbolize their experiences through art, language, dramatic play, music, and movement. Opportunities to use materials imaginatively and creatively.	If the children take a trip, they can be encouraged to discuss the experience, and the teacher can write down some of what they say. They can also reproduce some of the sounds they heard with rhythm instruments, or they can make a mural of their visual impressions, or recreate the experience with blocks.
Are developing the ability to deal with complex, abstract ideas.	Opportunities to note similarities and differences between things around them. Opportunities to sort, group, categorize, and classify the things around them.	At a group time, the children can be asked, "Who is wearing pants today?" "Who is not wearing pants?" The children can be asked to compare any two pieces of clothing from the housekeeping area in terms of color,

size, or function. A
box full of clothes
can be sorted in many
different ways. For
instance, the children
can put together all the
things that are worn on
the head or all the
clothes that have
stripes.

THE DEVELOPMENT OF CHILDREN'S THINKING

As you watch children grow, it becomes clear that there is a natural sequence of physical development. Children crawl before they walk, walk before they skip, and so on. The more that is studied about children's thinking, the clearer it becomes that there is also a natural sequence of intellectual development.

The psychologist Jean Piaget studied children for many years and found that their thinking progresses through certain stages.

Children's thinking is different from that of adults. A young child's mental abilities are different from those of even a child of seven. Efforts to push children beyond their abilities can affect their confidence and self-esteem, which in turn will affect their desire to learn and grow intellectually.

As is true of all aspects of development:

Intellectual development affects and is affected by all the child's other experiences.

The steps of development are different for every child, but the sequence is the same for all children.

The Stages of Intellectual Development

From birth to age seven, there are basically two stages of intellectual development.

The sensory-motor stage (birth to approximately age two) From the moment children are born, they use all their senses. They smell, touch, taste, hear, and see things around them. Their whole body is involved in their discoveries. At first, children make little distinction between inside and outside or between themselves and others. If someone comes when they cry, they feel good; if no one comes, they don't. In this stage, children live almost exclusively in the present. Everything is "me" and "now." Eventually, they separate themselves from the objects and the people around them.

The preoperational stage (approximately age two to approximately age seven) In this stage, children still need firsthand experiences, but they can begin to think about and compare things without having the real object in front of them. Words become clearly associated with specific objects or experiences. They become useful symbols—they are abstract and stand for concrete things. Pictures, dramatic play, and written words also become useful to children as ways of representing things.

While children become more familiar with symbols, their thinking is still very "sense-bound." They are often trapped by what they see. They will have difficulty holding an idea in their minds, or—as Piaget has termed it—"conserving" an idea. For example, children have little notion of the whole, once it is broken up into parts. They will think they have more cookies when a single cookie is broken into a dozen little pieces.

As another example, if you put a row of five cookies directly opposite another row of five cookies as shown below, a young child will say that both rows contain the same amount:

Row 1: 0 0 0 0 0
Row 2: 0 0 0 0 0

But if you then space the cookies in one row far apart, the child will most likely not remember what he just saw—that the two rows are the same—and will say that there are more cookies in the spread-out row:

Row 1: 0 0 0 0 0
Row 2: 0   0   0   0   0

These conclusions seem like mistakes to us, and yet they are natural for children of three. No matter how hard you argue, children will not change their minds until they are ready.

No matter how many times you try to "teach" children the correct answer, they will not understand it until they have reached the stage of development at which they *can* understand it. You might get them to *say* that a cookie broken into a dozen pieces is the same as a whole cookie, but they will probably do so just to please you. Forcing children to say something that they do not believe is true will only confuse them and shake their belief in their own abilities.

For the teacher, some implications of Piaget's observations and findings are:

What is important for the development of children's thinking is the variety of experiences they have and the opportunities they have at every

It is important for children to manipulate a variety of materials and make their own discoveries.

stage of their development to manipulate real things, and make their own discoveries with them.

Drills and adult-oriented activities are not the most effective methods of teaching. Children can learn some things this way, but much of it will quickly be forgotten.

If we want children to develop their ability to think, it is important to provide an environment which is rich in things to do, which changes often (but not too often), and which is filled with sensitive and resourceful people who respect—even marvel at—the process of intellectual development and the individual form it takes in each child.

In order to understand children and help them grow and develop, the ability to observe and record their behavior is among the first skills we must master.

We observe a child alone, in groups, with another child, and with adults; we observe the child at the beginning of activities, during activities, at the end of activities, and in between activities; and we observe the child in routine situations and at unplanned-for events. All are important. What we see, the child's nonverbal behavior, is just as important as what we hear, the verbal behavior.

People who work in human services find they need to sensitize themselves to observing nonverbal behavior. Just as we all learn to "tune out" dull speakers and many surrounding sounds, so do we learn to look without seeing. Try the following experiment in looking.

Find a tree and write a description of it. Don't read any further until you have written your description. Now check by reading further. Did you note that the bark is more than one color? There are darker and lighter areas. Also, the part that goes around away from you seems darker. The bark of some trees has a grayish hue. Some bark is very smooth. How did the trunk grow? Where was it wider? Was it straight, or did it curve? Perhaps it had many curves in it. What about the direction of the branches? Now the leaves. Go back out and see what you notice about the color, size, shape, and texture of the leaves. Be sure to see whether the young leaves are as dark in color as the older ones.

As you look at the tree, you may unexpectedly find yourself learning many things. If questions are raised in your mind, you will experience further learning as you seek the answers. Why do the branches thin out at the ends? Was the influence of the sun the only reason the tree grew in a given direction? Why did the tree bend differently from the way the one next to it did? You see how the natural development of the tree has been changed by the forces around it. If you were to draw the tree now, you might make it look rounder because you understand the effect of light on rounded surfaces. This observation has made it possible for you to begin to understand the tree and to understand also the role the environment plays in the growth of that tree. In a similar way we learn to understand children by observing them alone and during their interactions with other people and with things. This is the first step.

Nonverbal Behavior

The children are entering the classroom. How do they look as they walk in? Some children dart ahead of their parents. A little skip mixed in with running steps, and they are in the room. One child enters the room burrowing into her parent's body. Another child holds onto his parent's hand or leg. Some are hiding their faces. Each child is different. The

What does this child's nonverbal behavior reveal to you?

child's nonverbal behavior—the body movement, the posture, and the position of the head, legs, and arms—is meaningful. We often know as much about people from their nonverbal behavior as we do from what they say. A child may cry out to you, "I don't like you," and simultaneously push the child you are holding away and climb into your lap. His message really is, "I love you and I cannot share you."

Try these experiments in front of a mirror or with friends. Imagine yourself approaching a group who you think may not be happy to see you. Note the position of your body; note your walk.

Now approach the group knowing they are eagerly waiting to have you join them. Your shoulders shift, your arms and head change position, and your pace is different. You may even notice a change in your face.

Walk toward a full-length mirror feeling embarrassed, ashamed, proud, beautiful, or ugly. Note how your body reflects your feelings. Children's bodies and movements also indicate their feelings.

Teachers often notice changes in a child's appearance as the child becomes more self-assured in school. The ability to observe children's nonverbal behavior is a critical skill that you need to learn. That child who hovers around the housekeeping area and never enters it may be saying without words, "I want to play there, but I need a little help in order to join that group." The child who stiffens, jerks, and twists his fingers is showing you that he is tense or worried. The child who is near you all the time might be saying, "If you stay with me for awhile and help me join that group of children, I can begin to make friends with them."

Recording Presented Behavior

As you observe children, it is important that you learn to record what you see and that you not include diagnoses or value judgments in your report. A correct observational record might say, "He walked very slowly as he approached the activity; his shoulders were bent, his arms were down at his sides, and his hands were almost behind him. His head was down, and his eyes were looking upward." It would *not* be correct to record this as, "He timidly approached the group. Maybe he had a headache or a fever." If you say, "He is very intelligent," you have made a value judgment that is your opinion. It is meaningless for a teacher to make such statements. If you say instead, "He works puzzles with many pieces, he strings beads in such a way as to create patterns of color and shape, and he retells stories in sequence after hearing them once," you have written a meaningful report that will help you in your work with that child.

Using a Record of Presented Behavior

A teacher asked for help with Eric, who would play delightfully each day and then suddenly become enraged. He would hit other children, throw toys and blocks, and hit the teacher, who would try to restrain him. The teacher had no idea why this was happening. Eric would end each outburst by running out of the room. The teacher was asked to keep an anecdotal record on Eric, that is, to keep notes on his behavior throughout the day, including time, place, type of activity, and the interaction involved with the particular activity. Such an anecdotal record might read as follows: "8:40—Eric arrives and hangs up coat. 8:45—Eric stands near the cubbies, thumb in mouth, and watches the block area. 8:55—Eric slowly walks to the block area, and stands there for a few minutes; then he asks Johnny, 'Can I help you?' 9:25—Eric and Johnny build a repeat pattern of bridges."

When a five-day record was read, it was instantly noted that Eric acted out each day at about 10:45. It was also noted that this occurred regardless of the activity Eric was engaged in or the children with whom he was working. The teacher suspected that there might be some physical basis for this behavior, such as a low blood sugar problem. This was discussed with the school medical service. The teacher's guess was correct. Eric was helped medically, and the problem disappeared. The point is that the cause of his behavior might never have been identified without good observational skills on the part of the teacher.

The record might have shown that Eric became upset by any of a number of things—a certain child, a given type of activity, or a specific kind of interaction. Whatever the cause, the teacher needed information in order to help Eric to function. In Eric's case, another very important pattern of behavior was discovered through this anecdotal record. It was observed that Eric characteristically hesitated before joining an activity. He seemed to become quite tense in between activities. It was noted that a smile or a gentle pat from the teacher at these moments relaxed him and allowed him to move on to something else.

Some Things to Look For

In making this kind of observation, you could ask some basic questions about the child:

Does he always seek help, or can he solve reasonable problems himself?

Can he accept help when it is needed? You must describe behavior that indicates this, not just state your judgments.

Can he choose activities that interest him or pick the cookie he prefers, or does he want to be directed?

Does he always imitate what others do, or does he initiate things himself?

Does he grab things, or can he wait?

Does he seek approval for each thing he does, or does he derive satisfaction from the performance of a task?

How does he handle frustration, failure, anger, and joy in himself and in his peers?

How does he handle reasonable limits?

Does a dramatic change in his behavior pattern seem to occur on certain days or as a result of interacting with certain children or engaging in particular activities?

Always observe yourself, too. Do you interfere, or do you allow the children to make choices, to be independent, to solve problems, and to initiate activities? Do you accept the children's feelings and understand, for example, that they have a right to be angry and that your role is to help them find a socially acceptable way to handle their legitimate anger?

As you become increasingly familiar with child development and so-called developmental norms, your observations will become more and more meaningful.

Records

Not only do records help in evaluating children, meeting their needs, and following their growth, but they are also useful for conferences with parents and reports to doctors, speech therapists, and various kinds of clinics.

There are many kinds of formal and informal records. The teacher's needs and goals determine the kind of record he or she wishes to keep. Every schoolchild receives a record of academic growth on a report card. Many report cards also include an observational report on social and emotional behavior. Doctors keep a medical record and history on each patient, including height, weight, and other physical findings. When a child starts school, many records are kept concerning his birth, early life, family history, and medical history so that teachers can best plan for this child and be aware of the progress he makes.

As a teacher, you may find the following kinds of records helpful in different situations:

A *case study* includes detailed information about the history of the child and his or her family as well as a description of current patterns of behavior.

An *anecdotal record* is frequently used by teachers; it was described earlier. The teacher notes the child's behavior throughout the day and indicates the time at which she made each entry.

Checklists are also used. These are a series of statements; the teacher checks "yes" or "no" next to each statement or rates each one according to a specified number scale. For example: "Initiates own activity—(1) never, (2) sometimes, (3) always."

Observation helps the teacher learn that everything a child does is a significant fact about him: the number of puzzle pieces he is successful with, the length of time he can attend to a story, the painting he makes and the story he tells about it, the activity he selects or avoids, the way he handles himself with others and alone, his ability to communicate and the quality of his communication, and so on. All this information is important if the teacher is to plan for the full development of each child. Successful observation must include nonverbal behavior as well as things the child says; successful teaching requires good observational skills.

Suggested Observations and Questions about Children's Physical Development

Observe a child in the playground. Describe the child's use of her body. Does the child seem well coordinated for her age? If you elevate a balance board on its side, can the child walk across it? Does the child know how to jump, hop, and skip? Can the child throw a ball to someone? Can the child catch a ball thrown to her? Watch a group of children of different ages. Observe them doing the same kind of activity, for example, playing catch. Note the differences in their abilities and record them.

Observe a child in the classroom. Is the child able to cut with a pair of scissors? Can the child zip, button, and tie a knot or a bow? Is the child able to use the toilet independently? Does the child seem tired at any time during the day? When and why?

Suggested Observations and Questions about Children's Emotional Development

Observe one child. What seems to give him satisfaction? How does he show it?

What seems to make this child uncomfortable? Describe the situation. What was the child doing at the time? Was anyone else involved? Describe how the child acted.

Does this child outwardly express his agressive feelings? How does it make him feel to express these feelings? How does this child respond to outward expressions of other people's feelings of aggression?

Suggested Observations and Questions about Children's Social Development

Observe one child in the classroom. Does she make contact with anyone else? Who is it and what are the circumstances?

Does the child usually initiate contact with others or wait for others to come to her?

Does this child seem able to take turns? Describe a situation in which this did or did not take place.

Does this child seem helpful to other children? If so, describe one situation illustrating this.

How does this child relate to adults? Does she look to adults predominantly for protection, ideas for play, comfort, participation in play, or other things? Explain. Give examples.

Observe a child having a conversation with another child. Record the conversation. Did the children seem to express themselves easily or with difficulty? Did either of them give information, ask questions, or give directions?

Choose one child. When does this child talk most or least? What does the child talk about? Does this child talk on his own initiative, or does he need "prompting"? In what ways does this child use nonverbal means of communicating? Does he point, use gestures, etc.? Does this child talk primarily with other children or with adults?

Observe a child using blocks. Is the child haphazard in selecting blocks, or does she seem to choose blocks very carefully according to shape and size? Does the child seem concerned primarily with the construction itself or with the finished product? Is she concerned with construction problems like making a tower stand up or a block balance, or does it appear that working out some fantasy or dramatic-play idea is more important to her? How long does the child stay with this activity?

FURTHER READINGS

Bruner, Jerome: *The Process of Education*, Harvard, Cambridge, Mass., 1961.

Chukuvsky, Kornei: *From Two to Five*, University of California Press, Berkeley, 1963.

Freiberg, Selma: *The Magic Years*, Scribner, New York, 1959.

Hymes, James L.: *The Child under Six*, Prentice-Hall, Englewood Cliffs, N.J., 1963.

Stone, L. J., and J. Church: *Childhood and Adolescence*, Random House, New York, 1947.

3 THE CHILD IN SCHOOL

MEETING THE SCHOOL

During the preschool years physical, emotional, social, and intellectual growth are dramatic. The sleeping, crying, sucking infant develops into a child who speaks; who runs, jumps, and hops; who uses his hands to manipulate things; and who has many ways to express a variety of emotional responses. The baby, who makes little distinction between himself and the world around him, becomes a child who has a concept of himself in his family and community.

By the time children are three years of age, they have had a great many experiences and have already developed many abilities. If the child's first encounter with school is at this age, he or she must be acknowledged as a human being who has a distinct personality and who has definite likes and dislikes and definite strengths and weaknesses. Each child has many capabilities and many needs.

We often hear the question, "Is the child ready for school?" But it is just as important to ask, "Is the school ready for this child?" Some schools believe that the preschool program must focus on a child's social needs; others state that they are concerned with the child's intellectual growth. Still others believe that the school must be concerned with the whole child.

A program that has a curriculum which fosters the development of the whole child:

Sees growth as a complicated process in which physical, emotional, social, and intellectual development are interrelated

Provides a variety of firsthand experiences to allow the children to touch, see, hear, taste, and smell things in their environment

Provides for individual choice, experimentation, and discovery

Uses everyday experiences and materials as learning resources

Respects each child's interests, abilities, and skills

Provides continuity so that the children can build on experiences and develop understanding

Recognizes play as the child's method of learning about the world

A program that has a curriculum which seeks to develop human potential to its fullest provides opportunities for the children to:

Develop abilities and skills that give them a sense of competence and mastery

Feel unique and able to make a creative impact on the world

Develop mutually satisfying relationships with others

Develop problem-solving abilities and the ability to question and think critically

Learn to control their impulses while maintaining spontaneity and initiative

Channel their interests and energies into constructive activity

Become comfortable with their feelings

Express their thoughts and feelings in creative ways

Gain an understanding and working knowledge of the world and the people in it

See themselves as contributing members of a shared culture at home, in school, and in the community.

These program guidelines can help you understand the range of experiences children will have in an early childhood class. Parents have a need and a right to question educators about program guidelines. Teachers have the responsibility to explain clearly what they do and why they do it.

SEPARATION: THE ADJUSTMENT TO THE FIRST SCHOOL EXPERIENCE

When children start school, they are immediately involved in an important learning experience. They need to learn to move from the protection of their home to the outside world of school in which there are caring adults. The way a school handles the initial separation process is a reflection of the overall program goals.

Throughout life we face repeated separations—birth, going to school or camp, marriage, and death are all separation experiences. The way in which we learn to separate in early childhood can have an impact on later separations. This is one of the important relationships and interactions that affect our behavior. Can you recall some of your own feelings in past separations?

Can you remember how you felt the first time you went to school? Did you cry and feel you hated school? Perhaps you really wanted to go to school. Your siblings or friends were going. You also knew that your parents expected you to go. Nonetheless, you cried.

Can you remember your first day at college? Some of you came with friends, and together you found your way around the campus. Many of you came alone. If you did, you may have felt confused, lost, and frightened. At moments some of you wanted to turn and run.

Children's Different Experiences

Johnny cried for a week when he started nursery school. The teacher assured his parents that he would "get over it". She was right. The second week he cried for shorter and shorter periods of time. Eventually he stopped crying. It had worked—or had it? When Johnny started kindergarten the following year, he repeated the crying and eventually stopped. When he started first grade, he cried a little bit, complained of feeling nauseated, and then developed a tic (rapid blinking) in his eyes.

The tic left him at the end of a month. When he entered second grade, the tic reappeared, but this time it stayed.

Susan's mother stayed with her for two weeks when she started nursery school. Then she left the room for five- and ten-minute intervals. Eventually Susan was comfortable and adjusted to the separation. School was a successful experience. When Susan was six years old, the nursery school received a letter from her father. He had written to thank them. Susan's mother had been hospitalized, and he wanted the school to know that he felt Susan had been helped to manage this experience to a great extent because of the way she had *learned* to separate when she started school.

In her beautiful book *War and Children*, Anna Freud tells about the evacuation of children to the seacoast during the bombing of London.* The children's lives had been saved, but they were developing serious emotional problems. Arrangements were made to bring the mothers to the coastal shelters. The mothers stayed until the children were comfortable and familiar with the facility and the people in it. The mothers were then able to return to London and to continue their work for the war effort. The children were able to adjust to life at the coast. Many children who are called "school phobic" are afraid of separating from their parents, not of school.

The Primary Relationship

Parents are the source of life for the child. They provide food, care, and comfort. As the child grows, he should achieve some independence. He needs to begin to reach out. He stands alone, he walks alone, and he says "no" to test his own power. As he develops physically, emotionally, socially, and intellectually, he seeks out the world beyond his room, his house, and his street. He grows ready for a new adventure, school. Parents have a continuing problem during this growth period: When can my child go out to play alone? When can he walk without holding my hand? Can I slowly release my child? Can I separate from him as he enters school? Will the teachers judge me because of him? Will he love the teachers more than me? What happens to my life while he is in school? Can I trust the school with my child?

The Teacher's Role

The teacher must be sensitive to all the concerns that the parents have. She must understand that she is involved in one of the most basic

---

*Anna Freud and Dorothy Burlingham, *War and Children*, International Universities Press, New York, 1943.

learning experiences of the young child's school life. The child and the parents must learn to separate in a way that will have a positive impact on all parties involved. The teacher must understand the parents' needs and the child's needs. On the basis of these needs, she programs the initial school adjustment. It is important to realize that the child and parent who appear to have made a perfect adjustment to school are nevertheless continually dealing with it. Six months later the child may start bed-wetting or thumb-sucking because he is still testing the separation. A child who is very happy in school may wake up one day and firmly state, "I'm not going to school again." A child who is adjusted to school may become very anxious the first day the class goes on a trip or takes a walk. The articulate child will verbalize his fear: "Will Mommy know where I am if I go for a walk." How, then, does the teacher start the school year and meet these needs?

Preparing for Separation before School Starts

The teacher can begin to engender trust before school starts by arranging a visit for the parents and the children. Both the parents and the children want to see and become familiar with the premises—the playrooms, the bathrooms, the kitchen, the playground. The parents want to know the school's safety and health arrangements. They want to know what kind of person the teacher is—what she expects from them and what she expects from their child—and they want to know how to prepare the child for school. The child wants to become familiar with the school and the people in it. In short, the parents and the children want to know whether they can trust the school.

Preparing for Separation when School Starts

On the first day of school, the teacher needs to become familiar with each child and each parent. Is the child ready? Does he cling? Does he communicate? Does the parent hold him tightly and nonverbally communicate a sense of, "You don't want to leave me, do you?" Since the teacher cannot give the necessary personal attention to fifteen children, it is best to arrange for "staggered admission." Most schools start the term with five to seven children on the first day. This gives the teacher a chance to set up relationships with each child and each parent. The parent stays in the room. She holds the child when he wants to be held and lets him play when he is ready to play. She has been advised not to push the child away from her. The child and the parent stay for about 1½ hours. The child is directed to the open shelves, where a select and limited amount of equipment is stored. He is encouraged to choose anything he wants to play with and is helped to use the equipment in accordance with the classroom routines. Each child is given his own cubby and is told, "This is your cubby; no one else may use it but you. You may keep your things in it. It will be there for you every day." Something in that room becomes his.

Each day two more children are added to the group. The 1½ hour stay is gradually extended to a full school period. The teacher observes all the children. She sees their various reactions to the school situation and their different relationships to peers, to her, and to the equipment. She is aware of the parent reactions and the parent-child interactions. She may see moments of stress and note how these are handled. She observes the verbal and nonverbal reactions. Using all these clues, she is able to individualize the separation.

Separation: When the Child Is Ready

When the teacher feels the child is ready, she has the mother tell the child, "I am going out of the room for a few minutes, but I will be back." The mother may leave her coat as an assurance to the child that she will return. She never sneaks out when the child is absorbed in play. This would violate all trust. She stays out for a very few minutes and returns before the child is uncomfortable. The pacing of this delicate program is in the teacher's domain. She repeats these departures and extends their duration as she interprets the readiness of all parties. The children whose parents have gone home are not upset by the parents who remain. Some will say, "Johnny's not ready to have his mommy go yet." Some will try to help Johnny "Get ready." They remember how they felt, and they understand how their peers feel.

Children Help One Another

Ada had a difficult time adjusting to school. She was newly arrived in the United States and spoke only Greek. Her mother was bedridden. Her father had to start a new job. Ada's ten-year-old sister stayed in the room with her. It wasn't much help. Ada cried and seemed inconsolable. Then she spotted the guinea pig. The tears suddenly vanished as she cradled the animal and shared it with her sister. Ada was absorbed in the pig for a long time. The other children never questioned why Ada could put the animal in places that were off limits to them. She finally did adjust to school. Many months later a new boy started school. A child commented, "Look, he has his mother here." Ada looked up and said, in her newly learned English, "He is new; he needs his mama." Then she thought a moment and said, "I know—give him a guinea pig."

If a child does indicate that the parent is needed again, the teacher is sensitive to this need. Sometimes a word of reasurrance—"Mommy will be here" is enough. Sometimes she arranges for the parent to pick up the child early or to visit the classroom. The teacher and the parent have a common goal: the well-being of the child.

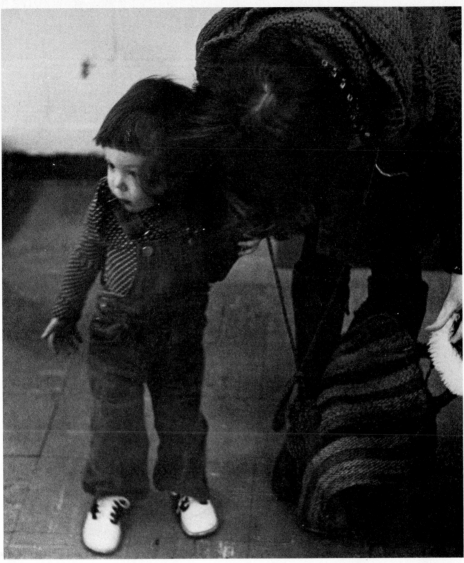

The parent tells the child she is leaving when the teacher sees that the child is ready to participate.

Difficult Situations

There are times when it is very difficult for a child to start school. If a new baby has arrived in the family, a child may feel he is being put out to make room for the baby. A parent is always advised to start a child's school experience several months before the birth of a new baby. Many family experiences can and do have a negative effect on a child's school adjustment.

Joe had an older brother who had been placed in an institution for brain-damaged children. Joe was positive that he had been brought to school to be left in the same way that his parents had left his brother. His mother sat in the classroom for a month. For a week he just sat on her lap. Then he played with toys that were at her feet. Finally, he slowly moved away from her seat at the back of the classroom and joined the other children. Yes, he made the adjustment. It was a vitally important learning experience for him. It meant many conferences and reassurances for his mother. It gave the teacher the most important reward of teaching—the feeling that flows from knowing you have done something positive and important for the mental health of a child and his family.

Another difficult situation arises when a parent cannot accompany the child to school during this adjustment period. Some parents explain that an absence from work could result in the loss of a job. They would sacrifice a day's pay for the health of the child, but not the loss of a position. Parents may have serious personal problems that make any visits to the school impossible for them. The teacher must find the best possible way to make the school adjustment a good experience for the family unit. When the child first attends school, he can come with someone besides a parent—a grandparent, another relative, or a family friend. This allows the child to feel that an adult whom he knows is with him in the new situation. This adult can then give the parents information about the school.

PARENTS IN SCHOOL

During the separation period the parents become increasingly familiar with the philosophy of the school. They might come to the school every day for as long as a week or two. This gives them an opportunity to observe the children using the play materials and interacting with one another and with the teachers. During this time many questions may occur to the parents.

"Why do they let the children get all covered with clay?" "Why isn't my daughter using the blocks the way the other children are?" "Why doesn't the teacher get upset when that child hits another child?" If possible, a comfortable room should be provided where the parents can meet with a warm, sensitive staff member, perhaps over a cup of coffee. This often helps to alleviate the parents' anxieties. If the parents are helped to feel secure in these initial days, they may be more comfortable discussing their questions with the teacher or director. This beginning adjustment period provides an excellent opportunity to encourage a dialogue between parents and teachers that will continue during their entire relationship. There will be times when a parent may want a private conference. The parent should feel that whatever is discussed will remain confidential. Parents should also be informed that the school will arrange for periodic conferences.

Interaction at the end of the day is important for parent and child.

   Schools often offer workshops for parents to help them understand
the curriculum of early childhood education. Workshops in block building, art, cooking, music and movement also provide parents with an

opportunity to share their knowledge and cultural heritage with teachers and other parents. This is an important way to enrich the program and have it truly reflect the needs of the children. Parents can also be helped to understand what their children are talking about when they discuss their school experiences at home.

Just as the classroom should be furnished appropriately to meet the needs of the children, so should the parents' room reflect and support the needs of the adult community. Books and articles relating to health, social services, and child development should be available. A bulletin board announcing local events and activities can stimulate parents and teachers to communicate their ideas and needs to one another. For some parents, the school might be the only place to which they can turn for information, referrals, job training, and the like. When a school sees itself as providing this kind of service, parents grow to trust the school more and more. This kind of trust has long-range effects; as the parents' trust in the school grows, the children's trust is also enhanced, and it is only through trust that real growth can take place.

DISCIPLINE AND SELF-CONTROL

We want each child to develop a feeling of competence and mastery. If we approach discipline as a way to control children and their behavior, then we are saying that someone has to have mastery over them. We must approach discipline with the realization that children need to learn *self-control*.

Here is an illustration of how discipline can work ineffectively. The children are sitting at a large table waiting for the teacher to bring the snack. There is a lot of discussion. The assistant teacher and the student are involved with the children. As the discussion goes on, the noise mounts. Some children shout to be heard above the growing din. The teacher walks in, stands at the door, and then yells, "This is supposed to be a quiet room. Stop this shouting!" The noise stops, but what has been accomplished?

The teacher has tried to reinforce a rule by breaking that very rule himself. He has also undermined the relationship between the children and the other adults. Yet such situations happen all too often. They are at best confusing to children.

The teacher in this scene may go even further. To punish the children, he may deprive them of their long-awaited snack and add, "I only give a snack to good children."

Does any of this sound familiar? Such an occurrence is not uncommon. Yet we all sense how unfair the teacher is being. He is condemning and punishing the children for something that he could probably have avoided by effective planning and handling.

Let's look at this scene to see what caused it and how it might have been prevented. Some questions come immediately to mind:

Why were the children asked to wait so long?

Why weren't the children involved in preparing the snack?

If the snack was unavoidably late, could the children have been involved elsewhere until it arrived?

If the children were already at the table, could they have been broken up into smaller groups, say, two different groups at different tables, each with an adult?

If the teacher wanted the children to be calmer before eating the snack, could he have gone over to the table, explained this to his co-workers, and asked them to work this out with the children?

Could the teacher have suggested to the assistant that he start a song that would calm everyone down?

With a gentle hand on one of the noisier children, could the teacher have calmly but audibly explained that the snack would be brought to the table as soon as everyone was quieter?

It often seems "magical" when a class runs smoothly with a minimum of disruptive situations or when a teacher can help calm an individual or group with a few well-chosen, softly spoken words. But there is no magic involved. "Good discipline" which sets clear limits that help children develop their confidence and self-control is based on some very basic principles.

How to Prevent Problems

Be a role model for the children The teacher needs to be a mature, sensitive, good-humored person who enjoys teaching—enjoys life— and can communicate this to other people. She is aware of her own feelings, needs, and desires as well as those of every child in the group. The teacher is firm, but gentle. She is warm and affectionate with the children and trusts their capacity to be loving and compassionate people.

The teacher's behavior needs to be consistent with her expectations for the children in her group. If there are rules prohibiting physical or verbal abuse and prohibiting loud noises when they disrupt the work of others, then the teacher has to observe them too.

The teacher also helps the children to accept the responsibilities of group life by demonstrating her own willingness to share them. For example, by participating in clean-up, she helps the children to recognize the necessity and importance of the job.

Establish a comfortable atmosphere The teacher knows that children are less apt to be disruptive when they feel secure and confident. She therefore shows respect for the children in her class and for their work. She provides enough time for them to become involved in what they are doing; she doesn't rush or pressure them. She recognizes that children need to assert themselves without always running up against the rules, and she allows for maximum individual expression within the limits of group life.

Encourage the children's independence   The teacher knows that children are less apt to be disruptive when they feel they have some control over their lives. She therefore allows for as much independence as possible. Many tasks that are part of the life of the classroom can be assumed by the children, such as setting up for a snack, taking care of pets, sponging tables, and getting paper and supplies.

It is also important to let the children make their own decisions whenever possible. They can choose their own activities during work time, pick the stories they want to hear, and help decide what foods to have for a snack.

At the same time, it will prevent problems if the teacher presents choices only when they are real. To ask a child, "Do you want to put your coat on?" when it is time to go to the park is to present a false choice and can cause unnecessary resistance.

Know the children in the group   The teacher needs to know the capabilities of the children in the group and then work *with* them and *not against* them. For instance, young children can't be expected to wait or sit for long periods of time. Asking the whole group to stand in line and be quiet before going to the park is often self-defeating.

Different children become angry, frustrated, or fearful in different situations and at different times. The teacher needs to respect these feelings while helping a child deal with them. The teacher needs to know when and why certain children experience conflict and how they may react.

For example, Johnny gets angry when he feels he won't succeed. In the past, frustration has led to his throwing toys on the floor, kicking over chairs, and hitting other children. Knowing this, the teacher tries to direct him to activities that have given him past success or to open-ended situations, or she sits next to him and presents him with possibilities for success with new materials.

There are also many children who find it difficult to go from one activity to another, and the teacher knows that such children need more guidance during the times referred to as "transitions."

Plan carefully   With a clear understanding of the strengths and weaknesses of the children in her group, the teacher needs to plan a program that will help develop feelings of self-worth and a spirit of group cooperation. When the children are actively involved in activities that are appropriate and enjoyable, there will be fewer disruptive occurrences. When a program includes a variety of activities and is scheduled to allow for differences in the children's styles and interests, things will go much more smoothly.

Each activity also needs to be carefully planned. For instance, if the teacher has planned a cooking experience, all the ingredients and materials should be collected before the activity begins. If she must leave the group to get a forgotten pot or spoon, this can be an invitation to trouble.

Set limits that are clear, reasonable, and consistent Children can be helped to accept rules and limits if the teacher keeps them down to a basic few, states them clearly in language she knows the children understand, and gives concise explanations of why they exist.

Children also need to feel that rules and limits are established in their interest and not for adults' needs alone. Rules will seem reasonable to a child if they are based on his or her safety and needs. Rules like this will help children feel more comfortable and secure and, in a way, will give them more freedom—they know they can be assertive without hurting themselves or others.

Children also need to feel that adults are reliable and fair. It is therefore important that the teacher be consistent in applying rules in the group. At the same time, children want to know that teachers are flexible and will take into consideration the particular individuals and the specific situation involved.

Emphasize what the children *can* do Children like praise for what they do. If they receive attention only when they misbehave, it is likely that they will continue this behavior. The opposite is also true. If children feel their constructive efforts are recognized and appreciated, they are more likely to pursue this course to get the attention they need.

Supervise effectively Timing is very important. If the teacher knows the children in his group, observes them carefully, and tries to be aware of all that is happening all the time, he can step into a situation *before* it becomes a problem. For example, the teacher sees Carol trying to carry a bucket of water filled to the brim. By offering a helping hand, the teacher can prevent the water from being spilled, children from slipping, and Carol from feeling inadequate.

The teacher can also help by stepping into a conflict situation *before* the children lose control. For example, the teacher sees Mary and Ellen tugging at the same truck. She feels that these children are not going to resolve their dispute by themselves.In this situation, she knows it is better to intervene and help the children before their tensions escalate and they get much more upset. To do this, the teacher must learn always to position herself in such a way that she has the best possible view of all the children, all the time. Her ears must become sensitive to all unusual sounds or changes in voice quality in the group.

What must the teacher know about these children in order to decide whether to intervene or let them solve their own problems?

In order to help prevent problems from occurring, the teacher needs to be free to go over to the children, to talk with them on their eye level, and to be able to touch them and possibly hold them and guide their actions. Shouting from across the room, "Tommy, don't knock down Judy's building," will have little effect on redirecting Tommy's actions.

What to Do When Problems Occur

Despite the many ways we have of preventing problems, they will occur. What then? The goal of discipline is to help children achieve self-control. Self-control is learned. When we say to a child, "Do not do that," we are

4 THE CLASSROOM

ROOM ARRANGEMENT

As you observe and work in classrooms, you will notice a great variety in the way the materials and equipment are arranged. You may also sense that each classroom has a different effect on you. Some classrooms may make you feel depressed, others, alert and alive. Some classroom designs seem to have a calming effect; others seem to overstimulate everyone.

You may remember classrooms where the teacher sat at a large desk in front of the room and you sat in a small seat filed in a row. Even if the teacher kept repeating, "I want you to feel comfortable here and ask questions whenever you want," the room told you, "Be quiet, you are a passive recipient of knowledge from above." The design itself created a distance between you and the teacher. It was planned to reinforce the idea of a teacher as the supreme, unquestioned authority. On the other hand, when movable chairs are placed in a circle or when a group sits around a table, there is a different tone in the room and more people seem to participate in the discussion.

In the early childhood classroom the same thing happens. If the children are told to sit in oversized chairs and listen to what a grownup has to say, this will influence their behavior in one way. Yet when the children can move freely in a room that has child-sized furniture arranged in a flexible and creative design, the room seems to say, "You are part of the learning process that takes place here."

Effects of Room Arrangement

The room arrangement will directly affect the children's behavior. For example, a room that looks like a child-sized toy cafeteria, with all the furniture lining the walls, will encourage the children to keep moving around (there may be a lot of running). They may go quickly from one activity to the next and hardly ever concentrate on their work. The vast, unfocused array of materials in this design may also overwhelm some children. On the other hand, grouping materials into well-defined areas will help the children make choices and become involved in their work. With this type of room arrangement, the children are encouraged to explore as well as concentrate on their work. It allows for movement from one activity to another, and at the same time it lessens the possibility of distraction. With this type of room arrangement the teacher can be an "enabler" who observes, who waits to enter into the play at the "critical moment," and who does not impose on the activity. He can be involved with one group or with an individual while still having a sense of the entire classroom. The movable furniture also makes it possible to rearrange the design whenever necessary. The teacher can make one area smaller and another larger, and he can move tables away from an area, depending on the group's interest and activities.

In this type of room arrangement, the equipment and materials are grouped into areas according to the manner in which they are used. These are called "work areas" or "interest areas." They provide comfortable work space. They are inviting and stimulating places for learning and fun.

Work Areas in an Early Childhood Classroom

Housekeeping area The equipment and materials in this area present many opportunities for the children to learn about the world around them. Included are furniture, dress-up clothes, and a variety of accessories that will help the children play the roles they see at home, at school, and in their community. Tools, stethoscopes, dolls, hats, telephones, and other props stimulate the children to assume such roles as those of parent, baby, teacher, hospital worker, plumber, and firefighter. Most often the entire area is designed to look like a house, but it can be a shoe store, a supermarket, a clinic, or any other place where children spend their time.

Block area Blocks are a basic part of the early childhood classroom. They provide a variety of learning experiences. Block building encourages muscle coordination, sensory discrimination, and eye-hand coordination. Playing with blocks can provide possibilities for problem solving in

Clearly defined areas facilitate an environment for learning.

A rich variety of shapes and sizes of blocks, in a large area away from traffic, allows for constructive, creative building.

mathematics and science and for language development. Blocks provide children with an opportunity to re-create their environment and clarify their ideas about how other people live. This kind of activity relates to social studies learning.

This area includes a set of hardwood unit building blocks that are very carefully designed to be in mathematical proportions to one another (Figure 4-1). For instance, the unit block is half the length of the double-unit block, but it is the same width and depth. The blocks are unpainted and sturdy. The basic shapes include squares, rectangles, and triangles. This area would also include toys that the children can use in their constructions, such as colored blocks, small trucks and cars, and rubber figures (about 6 inches high) of people and animals. These are called "block accessories." There might also be a set of large, hollow wooden blocks or large cardboard or styrofoam blocks with which the children can make such things as cars, spaceships, and fire engines to use as part of dramatic play.

These blocks and accessories need to be stored on low shelves so that they are easily accessible. The blocks should be arranged so that the differences in shape and size are apparent (Figure 4-2). For example, the unit blocks should be stored lengthwise. The block area needs to be protected and away from the main traffic of the room. At the same time,

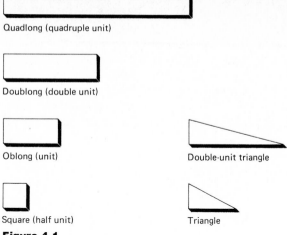

Quadlong (quadruple unit)

Doublong (double unit)

Oblong (unit)

Double-unit triangle

Square (half unit)

Triangle

Figure 4-1
Basic shapes of blocks.

there needs to be sufficient space to accommodate the children, working alone and in small groups, as they explore the many possibilities inherent in this material.

At any one time, a group of children can be collaborating on a complex highway that includes bridges and overpasses with houses and stores along the side of the road, while another child can be working alone discovering the mathematical relationship of a small block to one twice its size or experimenting with balancing a tower of double-unit blocks.

Figure 4-2
Storage of blocks. (a) Shelves with silhouettes of blocks on the back. (b) Blocks stored according to size and shape.

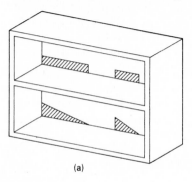

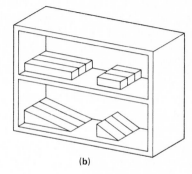

(a)

(b)

Area for manipulative toys and small-group games (table toys) The materials found in this area include puzzles, pegs and pegboards, stacking toys, beads and strings, and other toys that develop eye-hand coordination, small-muscle coordination and concepts of size, shape, color, and the relationship of the parts to the whole. There might also be games that are usually played by a small group of children—lotto, dominoes, and the like. Some materials in this area may require a "solution"; others, like Lego and table blocks, are more open to children's ingenuity and creativity. But all these toys are challenging and fun.

Work with these materials requires relative quiet, and this area should therefore be enclosed and separated from the active play areas. There should be tables and chairs in this area and perhaps small rugs on the floor. The furniture or rugs need to be reasonably close to the storage shelves. This makes it possible for the children to carry the materials to the tables or rugs without too much spilling.

Art area In this area there should be a supply of crayons, moist clay, paint, brushes of various sizes, sponges, scissors, and paper of different textures, sizes, colors, and shapes. At different times the open shelves in

Children can be independent when they know where to get and return equipment.

this area would also provide a variety of materials such as found objects, wire, bits of cloth for making collages or gluing onto boxes, and pieces of wood for constructions.

There should also be tables, easels, and room on the floor for children to work alone with these materials or on group projects. Some materials are available every day, while others are presented as a special project for the day or the week.

This area should allow children a maximum amount of exploration within clearly set limits. All the surfaces should be easy to clean, and whenever possible the art area should be near a sink.

Science area   Children enjoy collecting, studying, sorting, observing, and taking things apart and finding out how they work. The science area

Children's collections are part of the science area.

should provide things like shells, seeds, plants, magnifying glasses, and microscopes. Old radio parts, batteries, and books relating to specific areas of science are also included. Children also enjoy taking care of animals; thus gerbils, guinea pigs, and fish make valuable additions to this area. Depending on the variety of materials provided, the science area can be centered on a small table or can be expanded to a part of the room where the children will have enough space to explore the materials fully. Plants having different light needs should be put in many places around the room.

Water-play area Basins of water can be provided as part of the house-keeping area, but they can also be set up in a separate place. Large baby baths or special tables built for water play can be filled with water, and containers of various sizes with different-sized openings can be provided. Food coloring and soap flakes can also be added to the water. The children can wash dolls, toys, and furniture. For further exploration of weight, texture, quantity, and capacity, you can add straws, funnels, tubes, eggbeaters, and squeeze bottles.

Sand area In some early childhood classrooms there is a sandbox that is big enough for three or four children to use at one time. In others, a large basin or sand table can be filled with sand and accessories such as strainers, shovels, and funnels that expand the play and learning possibilities. Some schools alternate coarse salt with sand in this area.

Woodworking area Initially, the woodworking area can contain a sturdy table, a supply of wood and nails, a hammer, and some sandpaper. Later the teacher can add clamps, saws, pieces of leather, wire, and wheels for more complex work. A nearby pegboard with silhouette markings of the different tools can serve as a good storage place for the tools when they are not in use (Figure 4-3). It is important to have this area isolated and to have an adult available to help the children learn the proper use of the tools.

Music area In a certain designated part of the room, rhythm instruments such as bells, drums, and tambourines, as well as a phonograph and records, can be provided for the children's use. A pegboard or a table is a convenient place to store these materials. The instruments should be within the children's reach. Found "sound" objects and a tape recorder can also be provided.

Library area This is a quiet, well-lighted area of the room where the children are offered a carefully chosen selection of books suited to their age and interests. Also provided are rugs, rocking chairs, couches, or anything else that will make this a comfortable reading area for one

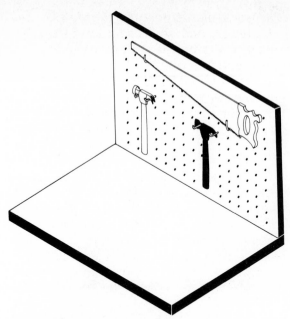

Figure 4-3
Woodworking table and pegboard with silhouettes of
tools for easy clean-up.

child or a small group of children. Some books are laid flat so that the
covers are exposed. Some stand open with an interesting picture displayed. The selection of books is changed whenever appropriate; magazines and pictures of special interest are included so that the children
will continue to find this an interesting and inviting area.

Relationships between Interest Areas

Interest areas are places where the children can find things that will
stimulate certain ideas. Yet many of the materials cannot be confined to
one area if maximum learning is to be achieved. For instance, art
materials may be involved in making a tree for a road in the block area,
or musical instruments may be part of the play in the housekeeping area.
It is also helpful for the children to find books about trucks in the block
area, books about families in the housekeeping area, and so on.

Placement of Interest Areas

The placement of the various interest areas depends on the answers to
some basic questions:

When books are attractively displayed and easily accessible, children find the library an inviting place.

Does the play in an area generally require quiet or active discussion and movement? For example, children are usually involved in active dramatic play in the housekeeping area, while they are relatively quiet in the library area.

How much seclusion does the play require? For example, the woodworking area needs to be in a protected space, while the music area can be much more open and near other activities.

What kinds of play add to one another, and what kinds detract from one another, when they take place at a close distance? For example, children involved in dramatic play go back and forth from the housekeeping area to the block area, but the sound of woodworking will severely limit the concentration required in the library area.

Which areas require water for play or clean-up? For example, the art area and the water-play area need to be closer to a source of water than, say, the block area does.

Which area requires the brightest light, and which is the best-lit part of the room? For example, the library area, where children are looking at books, needs stronger light than the housekeeping area.

Other Elements in Room Arrangement

The locations of the different interest areas form the bare skeleton of the room arrangement. Other elements that go into establishing a successful learning environment include the following.

Size of each area   The woodworking area is appropriate for two to four children, whereas six children can be part of dramatic play in the housekeeping area.

Condition of equipment   Toys and equipment in need of repair communicate a sense of disrespect for the materials.

Storage of materials   All materials within the children's reach should be for their use. Otherwise, the teacher spends too much time being the "director" of what is and what isn't for the children's play. At the same time, all toys and equipment not for the children's use should be out of sight so that the children are not distracted by these materials.

Traffic patterns in the room   Children like to feel they are inside an interest area, such as the housekeeping area or library, and can enter or leave it without walking through another child's block construction.

Variety of materials   A stimulating environment provides a well-chosen selection of materials that offer many choices without overwhelming or confusing the children with an overabundance of materials. New groups of children will function better if the teacher starts with a careful selection of a small variety of materials.

Display of pictures and the children's work   A few pictures displayed at the children's eye level can provoke a lot of interest and discussion. The pictures should reflect the children's lives and experiences. Displaying the children's work on the walls also makes them feel that they have had a part in shaping the environment. It makes them feel more a part of the group and helps give them a sense of self-worth. It is important that both the children's work and other pictures be displayed attractively and changed often. It is wise for student teachers to start saving pictures from magazines so that they can accumulate a good selection for classroom use.

Use of color   It is recognized that different colors affect us differently; yellow and orange are clearly more stimulating than blue, for example.

Evaluating a Room Arrangement

In evaluating a room arrangement, it's helpful to imagine that you are a child standing in the center of the room. What do you see as you look around? Is it a frightening and cluttered jungle of shelves, boxes, toys, and month-old paintings, or is it a comfortable room where you know which places are for running, which are for climbing, and which are for relaxing? Can you find the hammer that goes with the hammer-and-nail toy, and are there five pieces to the five-piece puzzle? Is there a balance between interest and order?

A good room arrangement promotes development of initiative and independence. Every child needs to know where to find what he or she needs with minimal adult assistance. For instance, when the children want to paint, is everything they need right there—smocks, paint, paper, sponges, brushes, easel (or other designated surface)? If the children want more paint, is it in small manageable containers or in large, clumsy glass bottles that will inevitably spill or break? Are the block shelves marked with large tracings of each shape so that the children can easily put the blocks back after using them? Keeping equipment and materials in approximately the same place all the time will also help the children to get to know their way around and feel secure in the environment.

Another way to evaluate a room's design is to observe the behavior of the adults and children in it. The room arrangement can demand teacher intervention and teacher-oriented activities, or it can guide the children to self-initiated discoveries. It can also prevent or create discipline problems. For instance, if Johnny has to walk through the block area to get to the bathroom, he will be more tempted to knock down Sarah's block tower than if she were building in an enclosed, protected area of the room.

The room arrangement says a lot about the way the teacher feels about the children and what he expects them to learn. It can help or hinder the teacher in fulfilling the aims of a planned program.

EVALUATING THE EFFECTIVENESS OF A LEARNING ENVIRONMENT

Observing a variety of classrooms can give you an idea of the different possibilities for arranging a classroom. Here are some basic questions you can use as a guide.

General Reactions

What is your initial reaction to the room? Does it seem sterile? Is it orderly or cluttered? Is it child-centered or teacher-oriented? Does it seem comfortable, cheerful, warm, and safe? Does it reflect a particular philosophy?

Physical Environment

Are there any inherent physical difficulties in the room? Are these temporary quarters? Is there water in the room? Is there enough space for the number of children? Are there bathrooms?

How has the teacher overcome or adapted to any physical difficulties in the room? Has she restricted or eliminated activities, or has she found inventive solutions? Do these solutions make it harder or easier for the adults and the children?

Interest Areas

Housekeeping area   Is the furniture arranged so that there is enough room for the children to move and play?

Does there seem to be a special place for everything? Are the materials easy to get at? Is clean-up easy? Is the equipment varied and exciting enough so that play can be interesting?

Do the dress-up clothes include materials that the children can adapt to their own desire? Can the materials be used by both boys and girls? Are accessory materials available which offer options for the children in playing a variety of roles?

Is water-play equipment provided? Is the equipment changed frequently so that the children can have many learning experiences?

Block area   Is there adequate room for building? Are there an adequate amount and variety of blocks for children at this age level? Are block buildings used for dramatic play? What is the overall quality of the play in this area?

Are the blocks arranged on the shelves so that the children can easily find the different shapes and sizes? Are the shelves overcrowded or orderly? Do the children have to crowd around one shelf to get a supply of all the sizes of blocks, or are the blocks distributed on more than one shelf in the area? Is there a tracing of each block shape on the shelf so that the children can easily replace the blocks during clean-up?

Is the block-building space protected from the other activities in the room?

Is there an adequate supply of accessories (trucks, cars, small animals, people, etc.)?

Do boys *and* girls use this area?

Does the teacher enter this area to work with the children?

Area for manipulative toys and small-group games (table toys)   Is there a sufficient variety of materials?

Are the materials appropriate to the children's age level and different abilities?

What is the general condition of the materials?

Do these activities seem to be busywork, or are challenges presented?

Are these toys near the place where they can be used?

Is this area arranged so that there is adequate space for the children to work undisturbed?

Are the toys arranged on the shelves in such a way that the children can get them easily and put them away without difficulty?

Art area   Is this area set up so that the children can work undisturbed by other activities?

Can the children generally help themselves to the equipment? Do they know where to find what they need?

Is clean-up easy for the children?

What materials are provided? Do they offer a variety, give the children choices, and seem interesting?

Is the clay soft enough for the children to use? What is the consistency? Are tools provided, or will the children use their hands? Is Plasticine or play dough offered instead of clay?

Is there adequate space for painting? What color paints are provided? Are the children encouraged to mix colors? What is the condition of the easels, the paint, and the entire area? Can the children put on and take off their smocks without the teacher's help? Are several widths of paintbrushes offered? Are the brushes in good condition? Is there a place nearby where the children can dry their paintings?

Is a variety of materials provided for making collages? Are the materials of different colors, sizes, shapes, and consistencies (hard, soft, rough, smooth)? How are they made available? How do the children seem to react to working with the materials and to the finished product?

Are other materials set out so that the children can handle them without adult help? What materials are provided for other activities, such as sewing and making mobiles?

Does the teacher insist that the children work on a special project, rather than let them choose their own projects?

Is a table set up at which the children will find a new activity each day? How much is this area the focus of the room? Is this where the teacher places herself? How many children work here at one time? How long does the activity last? What seems to be the purpose of the activity? Do the children avoid the other areas because they feel it will please the teacher if they stay here with her?

Science area   Are there materials available for experimentation? Are the displays formal teacher-made exhibits, or have the materials been gathered together, added to, and amended by the children? Is the teacher helping the children to understand the science learning found in all curriculum areas?

Woodworking areas   Is this area set up for work, or is it used for storing paper and paintings, etc?

What tools are available? Are they of a good quality? Do the saws cut? Are the tools the appropriate size for the children?

What type of wood is provided? Is it too hard?

Is this area well situated? Is it set up for maximum safety? Is it out of the traffic area?

Library area   Is this a comfortable, cozy area? Is there some relative quiet? Is this area removed from traffic? Is it away from noisier areas? Do the books seem appropriate for children at this age level?

Does the selection of books seem to reflect the children's interests? What is the quality of the selection? Are there books for research and information?

What is the condition of the books?

How are the books displayed? Does this seem to be an inviting place for the children?

Are the books placed near where they will be used? Is there a comfortable place to look at the books? How many children can use this area?

Things in the Room That Help Develop the Children's Self-Image

Is the children's work displayed attractively and with some care? Is the children's art work labeled with their names? Have stories that the children dictated been written down and placed near their work?

Are there charts or stories that relate to the children's experiences?

Are there photographs of the children?

Do the pictures, books, and other materials relate to the children's lives?

Do the materials reflect a multicultural world?

Is there some place for each child to keep his or her work, such as a cubby or a box labeled with the child's name?

Is there a mirror in the housekeeping area? Are there dress-up clothes for both boys and girls?

Do the materials in the room present equal options for both girls and boys?

Do routines seem well established so that the children can feel independent?

Are equipment and clean-up materials available so that the children can work independently and successfully?

Total View of the Classroom

Does the room arrangement promote a natural flow of activity?

Are the different areas self-contained, or do the children have to take materials from one area and go elsewhere to work with them?

Does the setup promote independence, or is an adult needed to initiate activity?

What areas are not used by the children? Why do you suppose this is so?

Is there a balance between comfortable, cozy areas where the children can work and relax and areas for more active play? Is there a balance between places where a child can be alone and where he or she can be part of a group?

ROOM-ARRANGEMENT KIT

The room-arrangement kit (Figure 4-4) will give you a chance to try out some of your ideas about room arrangement. It contains drawings of classroom furniture that you can cut out and arrange in many different ways.

Most commercially made furniture for early childhood classrooms comes in multiples of 6 inches. Tables are usually 24 inches wide by 30 inches long, 24 inches wide by 48 inches long, or 24 inches wide by 60 inches long. Storage cabinets and shelves are usually 12 inches deep by 48 inches long.

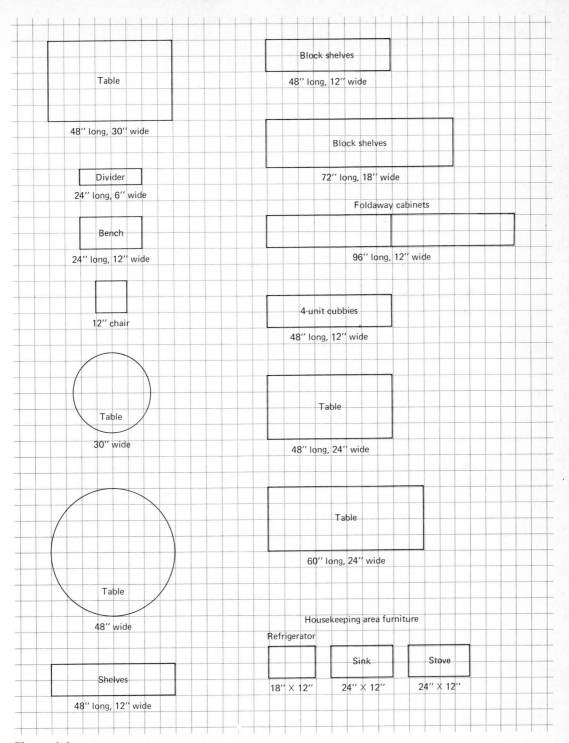

Figure 4-4
Room-arrangement kit. Scale: 1 square = 6 inches.

All the furniture shown in Figure 4-4 is drawn to scale so that a 6-inch-square area in real life equals 1 square on the graph paper. For instance, a standard-size chair that has a seat 12 inches wide and 12 inches deep is drawn two squares wide and two squares deep. A standard-size table that is 24 inches wide and 48 inches long is drawn four squares wide and eight squares long.

How to Use the Kit

Cut out the shapes and mount them on lightweight posterboard or cardboard. Feel free to add other pieces of furniture. You will definitely need additional shelves and dividers.

Draw the dimensions of a classroom to scale on another piece of graph paper. For instance, a room that is 25 feet wide by 30 feet long, or a total of 750 square feet, would be drawn fifty squares wide by sixty squares long.

Indicate any doors, windows, bathrooms, and sinks in the room.

Next, decide on the general placement of interest areas. Then move the furniture around on the graph paper until you feel you have a successful room arrangement.

Is there another design that works as well?

Keep the furniture in an envelope so that it can be used again. Have Fun! Experiment!

FURTHER READINGS

Beyer, Evelyn: *Teaching Young Children*, Pegasus Press, New York, 1968.

Goodell, C.: *The Changing Classroom*, Ballantine Books, New York, 1973.

Hawkins, Frances: *Logic of Action*, Random House, New York, 1969.

Howes, Virgil: *Informal Teaching in the Open Classroom*, Macmillan, New York, 1974.

Jackson, Phillip W.: *Life in Classrooms*, Holt, New York, 1968.

5 LEARNING IN THE CLASSROOM

HOW THE CHILD LEARNS ABOUT THINGS

In order to understand the curriculum, we must first recognize how children learn. The learning process is in many ways similar for all of us.

What happens when someone gives you something to eat that you have never seen before? If you take it at all, you will probably examine it, smell it, ask questions about it, and perhaps cut it open. If you are really feeling brave, you may taste it.

You use your senses. You see how this new thing fits into what you already know. You see how it is similar to, or different from, things that are familiar to you. You form an idea about it and then figure out what you're going to do with it. This is basically the same process a child goes through.

Let's use an apple to show how a child learns about things. In order to fully understand what an apple is, the child must have opportunities to learn about its various characteristics:

Color.
Size.
Shape and structure.
Function (what you can do with it).
Relations (who uses it; where it comes from).
Fabric (what it is made of).

The young child does this in three ways:

1 By using the senses.
2 By matching and comparing it with other things.
3 By sorting and grouping it

Let us examine each of these ways in turn.

1 Using the Senses

For the child to learn about this thing, an apple, he first has to use all his senses—sight, taste, touch, smell, and hearing—to examine it, manipulate it, use it, and hear about it.

When the child is given an apple, he will use all his senses to see that it is red and shiny, to feel that it is hard and smooth, to taste it, to smell it, and to hear what it sounds like when it is chewed. All these sensations (even without the words to express them) will add up to the child's idea of an apple. Hearing the word *apple* or any words that describe his experience will give him additional information that he will associate with this new idea.

78

2 Matching and Comparing

The child also has to have opportunities to see the similarities and differences between this new thing, an apple, and known things in his world. Each new experience will either fit or not fit into his new idea. For example, eating another red apple will fit into the idea. If the second apple is bigger, redder, or shinier than the first, it will expand the original idea of an apple. A green or yellow apple will modify the original idea even further.

Then the child comes across a tomato. He may first try to fit it into what he already knows. He may even call it an apple. But through repeated and different experiences with this thing, he finds that it is easier to squeeze than an apple. If he sees the inside, he discovers that it is red, not white, and that the seeds are white, not black. People around him are also calling this thing something else besides an apple. In time, he learns that it is *not* an apple, and he forms a new idea, that of a tomato.

The child also learns that the apple is not like other things—such as a brown, straight-backed chair—in many more ways:

AN APPLE	THE TOMATO
The apple is red.	So is the tomato.
The apple is juicy.	So is the tomato.
You can eat it.	You can eat it.
But	
The inside is white.	The inside is red.

The child also learns that the apple is not like other things—such as a brown, straight-backed chair—in many more ways:

AN APPLE	A CHAIR
The apple is red.	The chair is brown.
It is basically round.	It has straight lines.
It is edible.	It is not edible.

Thus the child needs opportunities to match and compare real things that are alike and not alike—the same and different—in a variety of ways.

3 Sorting and Grouping

Besides matching and comparing two things, the child also needs opportunities to sort and group things together. For instance, a collection of objects that includes an apple, a banana, a basketball, a round cookie, a red rubber toy, a wooden boat, and a yellow squash can be grouped according to:

COLOR

Red	*Yellow*	*Other*
Apple	Banana	Basketball
Red rubber toy	Squash	Cookie
		Boat

SHAPE AND STRUCTURE

Long	*Round*	*Other*
Banana	Apple	Red rubber toy
Squash	Basketball	
Boat	Cookie	

FUNCTION

Play	*Eat*
Red rubber toy	Apple
Boat	Banana
Basketball	Squash
	Cookie

Sorting and grouping objects can become more complicated if the categories overlap, with one object falling in more than one category. For instance:

Red Things	*Food*	*Other*
Apple	Apple	Basketball
Rubber toy	Squash	Boat
	Banana	
	Cookie	

The categories can also become more complicated if they include a combination of characteristics like:

Red Round Things
Apple

Implications for the Classroom

Exploring, matching, comparing, sorting, and grouping are all necessary for the child's cognitive development. These activities can take place in a variety of spontaneous and planned ways in the early childhood classroom. If we go back to the example of the apple, it can be dealt with in various situations.

Snack time   The children can cut it into pieces, count the seeds, taste it, and talk about it. Different kinds of apples can be presented for the snack. They can be compared and eaten and then compared with other foods.

Part of a cooking experience   The children can peel it, cut it, and watch it change when heat is applied to it.

Part of a lotto game   A picture of an apple can be matched to a real apple, to another picture of an apple, or to the printed word *apple*.

In the housekeeping area   The children can peel and cut real apples. They can also compare a real apple with a plastic apple and pretend to peel and cut the plastic one. If an apple is put in a bowl with an orange, a pear, and a banana, for example, the children can compare it with the other pieces of fruit.

In a book   The children can see both the word *apple* and a picture of an apple in many alphabet books. Books can also tell about how and where apples grow.

In a store   The children can go to a store and buy some apples. They can also find other things in the store that are made from apples, such as applesauce, apple jelly, and apple butter.

In a story   The children can make their own books about their experiences with apples: their trip to the store, a cooking experiences using apples, a snack that included apples, etc.

The process of conceptualization depends on the child's having many firsthand experiences so that he can:

Manipulate	Sort
Explore	Group
Experiment with	Question
Choose from	Hear about
Match	Talk about
Compare	

The Importance of Language

Language is an essential part of this learning process. Words help the child to retain information, expand learning, and deal with new concepts. The teacher can use and elicit language when the children are introduced to new things or when they are spontaneously engaged in activities. Some questions the teacher can ask that will aid or expand the children's learning are:

What does it feel like?
Does it smell like something you know?
Who is wearing something that is the same color?
How did you feel when you held the ice?
What happened to your eyes when you peeled the onion?
Why do you think the butter melted in the pan?
How do you keep yourself dry when it rains?
Why do you think your building fell down?
What can you do with it?

The children's answers to these questions give the teacher clues as to their information, lack of information, and misinformation. Their answers also give the teacher ideas about new experiences to plan for the children.

FURTHER ACTIVITIES FOR MATCHING, SORTING, AND GROUPING

There are many sorting and grouping activities you can use with children of different ages. These activities can develop skills necessary for understanding math, reading, and science concepts. The children's age and interests will determine what they use in an activity. Activities would include: real objects, then pictures of objects, then words.

In the simplest matching activities, the children can match real objects to real objects; children in a more advanced stage can match real objects to pictures; and finally they will match real objects to words.

Activities get harder as they go from the concrete to the abstract (matching real objects to pictures and words) and the simple to the complex (matching one characteristic to two or more characteristics).

Figure 5-1

Matching real things to pictures.

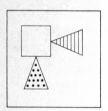

Matching Games

Matching real things to pictures   On cards, draw around wooden blocks and color the shapes the same color as the blocks. The child places the blocks on top of the appropriate block shapes. Using blocks, he may also be able to reproduce the pattern on the table next to the card (Figure 5-1).

Matching pictures to pictures   Make pairs of cards that the child can match (Figure 5-2). Matching designs can also be put on flat clothespins and tongue depressors (Figure 5-3).

You can also make this matching game using pictures of familiar objects. Just get two copies of the same magazine and mount matching pictures on pieces of cardboard.

Figure 5-2
Matching pictures to pictures: pairs of cards.

For older children you can use numbers, numerals, or letters (Figure 5-4).

Matching words to pictures Here each pair consists of one word with a picture and one card with a word (Figure 5-5a). The children can be aided by making the cards of interlocking shapes (Figure 5-5b).

Matching and comparing pictures The child is shown two identical pictures and is asked, "How are they alike?" The child is then shown similar but different pictures—two different cats, say, or two different bicycles. Then the child is asked, "How are they alike?" "How are they different?"

This kind of activity can be used throughout the day in spontaneous situations.

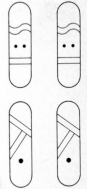

Figure 5-3
Matching pictures to pictures: designs drawn on tongue depressors.

Sorting and Grouping Activities

Using real objects

1 Put different objects on a tray or a table—for example, an apple, a banana, a pear, and a toy car. Ask the children, "Which one doesn't

Figure 5-5
Matching words to pictures.

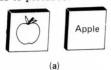

(a)

Figure 5-4
Matching pictures to pictures: numbers and letters.

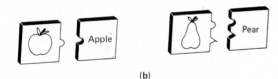

(b)

belong here? Why?" This activity can also be used in spontaneous situations throughout the day.

2 Put different kinds of objects on a tray or a table, for example, a small plastic lion, tiger, elephant, dog, and cat and a plastic apple, banana, and pear. Then ask the children, "Which things go together?" The children group objects, talk about why they go together, or both.

At first, a child may group all the animals or all the fruits. He can then be encouraged to group the animals according to whether they are farm animals or zoo animals.

3 Put pairs of objects on a tray or a table, for example, a knife and a fork, some paint, and a paintbrush, and a left mitten, and a right mitten. Then ask the children, "Which ones go together?"

Using pictures

1 Cut out several pictures of things we eat, things we wear, toys we play with, etc. Once the children know what is the common characteris-

Sorting and matching can be an absorbing activity.

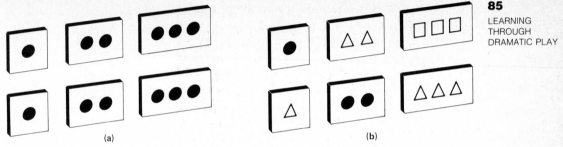

Figure 5-6
Sorting and grouping with pictures.

tic of each group, they are given two groups of cards and two boxes. They then sort and group the cards.

2 You can also put different amounts of dots, shapes, or pictures on cards; the children then sort and group all the sets with the same amount (Figure 5-6a).

If the children have difficulty sorting cards, you can put one from each group in a line on the table. The children then sort the rest of the cards accordingly. The cards can have different shapes as well as different pictures (Figure 5-6b).

Using words Explain that you are going to list things that are in a category—that go together—like fruits.

When you say something that doesn't fit in the category, the children are to tell you so or raise their hands. For example, say: "Banana, apple, pineapple, bicycle."

These materials and games are just samples of different matching, sorting, and grouping experiences for young children. While you can apply the general ideas presented here, such activities, like all others in the program, must be adapted to the individual child's needs and interests. For example, if Jack is interested in cars, he can match and sort model cars or pictures of cars. If Ann likes baseball, she can match baseball cards or sort them by teams.

LEARNING THROUGH DRAMATIC PLAY

Dramatic play is a child's way of dealing with the environment; it is a way of remembering experiences, exploring new things, and expanding ideas about people, places, and social relationships.

For the teacher, dramatic play is an excellent way to find out about children's concerns and misconceptions. It is also a way to provide activities that broaden children's understanding of the world around them. Observing dramatic play, adults get clues about children's most intimate thoughts and feelings. Children often use dramatic play as a way to unravel confusions and deal with the complicated process of growing up. One girl whose mother had just had a baby was often seen playing "Mommy" going off to to the hospital, coming home, and caring for the baby. She also wanted other children to take the part of the older sister and other family members; by assigning them certain tasks, she was, in a way, trying to find her new place in the family.

The things children watch on television are also of major concern. Children often play out the violence or war they see, or they may imitate a powerful superhero. Sometimes they will play "dead" and then get up and start all over again. In these cases, as with other instances in dramatic play, teachers have the responsibility to help children deal with the fears and confusions they may be expressing. It is also important for teachers who see recurring violent behavior in the classroom to help children find ways of feeling powerful without having to victimize or hurt other people.

Children also use dramatic play as a way of trying out the different roles of the people around them. As a way of understanding more about the world, children almost seem to get inside other people's skin. One teacher realized that she had underestimated a child's powers of observation when she suggested to a girl, "You be me." The child then gave a pretty good imitation, right down to her gestures and walk. Parents, too, learn a lot about themselves when they see their children play house.

In dramatic play, the most familiar roles are usually tried first. Children will be parents, babies, relatives, and even household pets. The activities they choose will most likely be the same ones they see around the house—cooking, cleaning, taking care of others, and being taken care of. Their excursions will be the most common ones, like shopping, taking a bus, or visiting a friend.

The housekeeping area is usually the center of these activities, and the dress-up clothes and props that are there can add to the play. Dolls, dishes, pots and pans, and cleaning equipment are the basics, but the addition of something like an ironing board and an iron will suggest new ideas. A construction hat, pieces of material, scarves, or a doctor's stethoscope, for example, can also trigger a variety of exciting dramatic-play possibilities.

Depending on the children's interests, the housekeeping area can be transformed into other places that are familiar to them. One group tried making it into a clinic. They turned over the refrigerator to make an examining table, and they covered some pieces of furniture and added others. With trips to a doctor's office and the neighborhood hospital, with many props provided by a father who was a hospital worker, and with a visit to the classroom by a doctor, the play became detailed and exciting.

Other possibilities for the housekeeping area include:

A shoe store
A dentist's office
A restaurant
A supermarket

Dressing up in adult clothes offers the child an opportunity to try out various social roles.

Often the children's imaginations can transform a very unstructured material like a large cardboard box into many different kinds of things. It can be a house, a boat, a fire engine, or a spaceship.

There are other ways that dramatic play can help the children understand the world around them. At a group time, they will enjoy pretending to be various animals or pantomiming activities they have seen or experienced, such as:

Blowing up a balloon
Peeling and eating a banana

Sometimes children follow patterns made by others. . . .

Going on a train
Visiting a zoo

The children can also use their natural talents to explore their emotions in response to questions like "How do you look when you're mad?" or "How do you show that you like someone?"

THE VALUE OF PLAY IN COGNITIVE LEARNING

Studies of growth and development have demonstrated that it is important for children to use their senses fully; otherwise, their learning may be impaired. Children have the opportunity to develop their senses through play. In play, they also learn who they are, they learn the roles of the people around them, and they become acquainted with the culture and the mores of the society. They begin to reason, to develop logical

. . . Sometimes children make their own patterns.

thinking, to expand their vocabularies, and to discover mathematical relationships and scientific facts.

Perceiving similarities and differences in play materials is basic to later procedural thinking. Simple activities like classifying buttons, making patterns with pegs, or using many other kinds of manipulative equipment develop visual discrimination, or the ability to distinguish differences and similarities in things that we see. This prepares the child to eventually see the differences between letters like *c*, *d*, *o*, and *p*. Playing with blocks helps children to discriminate sizes and shapes. Even when they sort and replace the blocks on the shelf, they are involved in basic learning experiences. As children work with puzzles,

Growing sprouts from mung beans provides a basis from which the teacher can extend the child's learning.

they further refine their perception of visual and spatial relationships.

Auditory discrimination, or the ability to distinguish similarities and differences in sound, is also developed through play. Music and movement activities help the young child develop listening skills. Movement responses to music require that a child listen carefully to discriminate between high and low, between soft and loud, and between various rhythmic patterns and moods. These differences are internalized, and the child responds with his body. Children also learn to discriminate sound characteristics by using sounds and words that are long and short or loud and soft. Rhyme perception is another helpful skill which can be taught through poems, word games, and songs. Children also learn to recognize similarities and differences in sounds by hearing the teacher's voice when he is reading stories and by listening to the quality and rhythm of certain words. Distinguishing variations in all kinds of sounds prepares the child for discriminating between the sounds that letters represent.

All these experiences demonstrate how essential play is if we want children to utilize all their resources and develop the skills they will need to deal with abstract problems. It is also clear that the more stimulating the environment, the more enriched children's conceptual and perceptual development will be.

The Teacher's Role in Play

Play alone is not enough. The teacher needs to sharpen the child's awareness and focus the learning. He cannot interfere with or dictate the discovery. He creates an environment for it. Aware of the potential in the discovery, he can define and present the problem that will facilitate learning.

The following example illustrates the teacher's role in stimulating the thought process that emerges from play. The teacher who has created the climate for learning by supplying and arranging the equipment sees a child playing with cars on ramps that he has constructed with blocks. She knows that if a car is placed on a slope made with blocks, the speed with which it descends and the distance it goes are affected by the slope and length of the ramp. She asks, "Johnny, why did this car go faster than that one?" She also introduces new words to his vocabulary—*slant, ramp, slow, faster, above, below, under, large, tall, smaller than*—and uses and elicits this vocabulary in conversation.

In order to refine the child's visual discrimination, the teacher does not work a puzzle for him, but helps him to see the connection between the shapes. When stacking blocks, the child must visually judge the size of matching blocks. When he is building a bridge, he discovers the need for two similar uprights. The teacher then discusses this. The teacher must realize that her role is not to do, but to enable the child to do and then to allow him to discuss what he has done, thereby making it a learning situation. An experienced teacher tries to talk less in order to get the children to talk more. She encourages them to ask questions, since learning should be the result of curiosity and a constant search for solutions. If successful solutions are found, the quest for further learning continues. Success begets success. A climate that allows for success engenders trust. To learn, a child must trust and feel a positive sense of his or her own worth.

Basic to the learning process is children's ability to trust themselves and the adults who teach them. This is totally interactional. Children must trust the people in their world, or else they reject all that these people want to teach them. They learn to have faith in those who respect them and accept their feelings. This allows children to find success. In turn, they learn to trust themselves. In a climate that engenders trust, they want to learn and are able to learn.

FURTHER READINGS

Biber, B., E. Shapiro, and D. Wicken: *Promoting Cognitive Growth: A Developmental Interaction Point of View*, National Association for the Education of Young Children, Washington, 1970.

Brearley, M.: *The Teaching of Young Children*, Schocken Books, New York, 1970.

Cass, Joan: *The Significance of Children's Play*, B. T. Blatsord, London, 1971.

Hartley, Ruth, Frank Lawrence, and Robert Goldenson: *Understanding Children's Play*, Columbia, New York, 1952.

Hess, Robert D., and Doreen J. Croft: *Teachers of Young Children*, Houghton Mifflin, Boston, 1972.

Schulman, Anne S.: *Absorbed in Living Children Learn*, National Association for the Education of Young Children, Washington, D.C., 1968.

6 THE CURRICULUM

THE INTEGRATED CURRICULUM

The curriculum includes all the activities in the classroom that are planned and provided for the children. The curriculum can be divided into the following seven subject areas.

Language arts This includes written and spoken language and the skills involved in prereading and reading.

Mathematics This includes number concepts, measurement, and geometry (which involves putting things in groups) and comparing the volume, weight, length, and area of things in time and space.

Science This includes concepts about the natural world such as growth, reproduction, and weather and concepts about the physical world such as sound, light, magnetism, and electricity.

Social studies This includes concepts about the child as a member of a social group and such topics as members of the family, people's work in the community, and things that people need to survive.

Music This can include singing, using instruments, and some basic musical notation, as well as movement and dance.

Art This includes the use of creative media involved in drawing, painting, collage, construction, etc.

Health and physical education This includes health and safety as well as activities for physical development such as exercises, games, and creative movement.

Rationale for Curriculum Development

Traditionally, programs developed so that each curriculum area was taught as a separate learning experience. Some schools allocated a percentage of time to be spent on each area, for example, 60 percent of the day for language arts, 15 percent for mathematics, and 10 percent for science. This sometimes meant that children sat and read a reader and then sat and read a social studies text and then sat and read some more. This structure helped administrators and inadequately trained teachers. Each curriculum area had a guide that stated the required learning level for each grade. Children were adapted to this guide. If you achieved the learning prescribed for a given grade level, you were a success, and the teacher promoted you. If you did not achieve the prescribed level of learning, you were a failure and were held over. With this approach, the curriculum does not flow from children's interests and needs. The child must become interested in the demands of the curriculum. The individuality of each child is lost. The curriculum guide is the dictator.

Today's teachers are trained in child development. They no longer need to adapt children to curriculum guides. They can now develop a curriculum based on children's needs. Teachers now have to be aware of the wide potential for learning in each activity. Then they will find that they are constantly enriching each experience.

Curriculum areas are not isolated; they are all interrelated and integrated with one another. An integrated curriculum means that the teacher is always aware that in any given activity there is the potential for learning in many curriculum areas.

Each area in the room can develop many curriculum areas. *For example, the housekeeping area involves opportunities for the following learning experiences.*

Language arts   In dramatic play, the children are constantly expressing themselves: "What do you want to eat?" "Where are you going?"

If the children "act out" a story with a beginning, a middle, and an end—like going to the store, doing the shopping, and coming home and cooking—the teacher can record the story in pictures, words, or both.

Signs can also be used in this area—reminders like "Buy milk" or labels like "Sink" and "Stove," for example.

Mathematics   There are many ways in which the children can group things in the housekeeping area. For instance, they can group all the kitchen utensils, all the dishes, all the hats, and all the shirts.

They can make play dough, which involves measuring and counting. Other cooking activities also involve mathematical concepts.

Science   In water play in this area, the children can discover different methods of making bubbles—with eggbeaters and straws and by swishing their hands in soapy water. They can see which things sink and which things float. They can also make a doorbell that works.

Social studies   Children can talk about and pretend to go on various trips—to the store, on a picnic, or to a friend's house, for example. They can talk about family members and what they do, and they can act out the various jobs of people at home and in the community.

Music   Many children use music spontaneously in this work area. A child will often sing as he works or puts a doll to sleep.

Songs that are appropriate for use in this area include "Clean-O" and "This Is the Way I Wash the Dishes" (or "This Is the Way I Put on Clothes").

Art   The children's artwork can decorate the walls of the housekeeping area. The children can also make things for the house such as curtains and doll clothes.

Health and physical education   Discussions in the housekeeping area can deal with topics such as health, nutrition, and sex education.

Learning in each curriculum area also takes place in many parts of the room and occurs throughout the entire day.
For instance, music can be:

Learning a finger play with a group of children
Making different sounds by banging blocks of various different sizes together
Singing "The Wheels on the Bus" when the children pretend to go on a trip

Mathematics can be:

Taking three cookies at snack time
Filling and emptying a container at the water table
Putting on a pair of mittens
Counting the steps on the slide in the playground
Talking about yesterday and planning for a trip tomorrow
Singing a song about six little ducks

The children can experience many curriculum areas in one activity.
For example, when making fruit salad, the children are involved in:

Going shopping for the different fruits and finding out where they came from (social studies)
Reading a recipe (language arts)
Cutting different fruits into pieces (mathematics)
Comparing different seeds (science)
Talking about the experience and recording their comments (language arts)

Curriculum areas can also be related by an idea or a concept that the children are developing. *For example, the concept of "big and little" can be learned by:*

Making different movements with the arms (physical education)
Eating crackers of different sizes at snack time (mathematics)
Using boxes of different sizes for construction (art)

The concept of "growing" can be learned by:

Planting and caring for seeds (science)
Measuring seed sprouts at different intervals (mathematics)
Writing a story about the things a baby can do and about the things the children can do now (language arts)
Reading *Look at Me Now**

A program that recognizes this interrelation of all the seven curriculum areas has an "integrated curriculum."

In order to help you see the scope of each curriculum area, we shall present them separately. This does not contradict our belief in the integrated-curriculum concept for learning.

LANGUAGE ARTS

Listening, speaking, reading, and writing are all part of language arts. This one term is used to emphasize the interrelationship of all these skills. Language starts with listening. Infants learn to distinguish and respond to the tone, quality, and mood of the voices in their environment. The infant uses many sounds that the parents learn to recognize as signaling anger, pain, and contentment. The vowel and consonant sounds that the infant uses while gurgling and crying are important, as well as the nature of the crying. As the parent and child play together, there is an interchange of sounds. Each repeats the other's sounds, and speech gradually emerges. The child learns the language of his environment. Jack's mother said "damn it" every time she dropped something. When Jack dropped something, he said "damn it" in the same matter-of-fact way that Susan, who was from a different home, said "I dropped it." Children learn words from what they see, hear, feel, touch, and smell when words are supplied for their experiences.

Early childhood school life exposes children to many experiences which can result in the use of more and more language. The teacher is a model and a facilitator of language. He uses language to reflect the children's experiences. He helps the children use language to express their reactions. The teacher encourages discussions at all times and helps the children to enhance their vocabulary with adjectives and adverbs. He might ask, "How does the grass feel?" The children might then respond,

"The grass feels soft, sticky, and pointy. . . ."

or "How does it look?"—to which the children might respond,

• *Jane W. Watson, Robert E. Switzer, and J. C. Hirschberg, *Look at Me Now*, Golden Press, New York, 1972.

"It is green, brown, and yellow; some blades are tall, and some are short; it bends. . . ."

The children learn that they can discuss their experiences and feelings. They also discover that the teacher can write down what they say and can read it back to them exactly as they said it.

What happens that helps us learn to read? We don't have the complete answer to this. We do know that reading is a process which involves thinking and must be learned. We also know that some skills must be learned before others can be mastered. This is referred to as the "sequential development of reading." Although reading is usually considered to be the recognition and understanding of written symbols, acquiring this skill depends on developing fully the sensory-motor skills from birth on.

The child dictates her story, the teacher writes it down, and then it can be read.

Prereading skills form the basic foundation necessary for the successful development of a reading program. Having children learn to read before they have developed this foundation often leads to reading difficulties. For the preschool teacher, this emphasizes the importance of play and the need to use play to develop the necessary reading skills. (See "Value of Play" in Chapter 5.) The following is a descriptive listing of prereading skills and how they are developed through play.

Language skills These skills include listening and speaking, and they involve both understood and used vocabulary. Language skills emerge from activities and experiences (not from drills). The development of these skills depends on the child's curiosity and on the help of supportive adults. A child assimilates a word if he needs it, and because of that need he uses it. Grammatical speech is learned as a child learns language. A child will not say, "Am girl I." She will learn to say, "I am a girl." Language development is aided when the adult treats the child and his language with respect. Teachers should not label slang expressions as wrong; instead, they can present alternative phrases. If children's speech is accepted, they will be encouraged to broaden their means of expression. Some ways for the teacher to develop language skills through play include:

1 Helping a child verbalize his or her play experiences
2 Reading and discussing stories
3 Dramatizing stories
4 Having meetings to discuss various topics, such as what the children do during playtime
5 Planning for, or following up on, a trip

Visual discrimination This skill involves the ability to distinguish differences in things that are seen. Being able to perceive differences and similarities is the forerunner of differentiating the letters of the alphabet. The development of this process takes place through such activities as:

1 Working with puzzles, pegs, beads, and blocks
2 Looking carefully at things in the environment—clouds, flowers, leaves, stones, sticks, and birds, for example
3 Handling, sorting, and talking about objects in terms of their similarities, differences, and individual characteristics

Auditory discrimination This skill involves the ability to distinguish differences in things that we hear. The development of this skill includes:

1 Coordinating body movement with high and low sounds or soft and loud sounds
2 Guessing who is speaking
3 Dancing and singing
4 Listening to the rain and the wind and identifying sounds coming from outside
5 Rhyming words and playing games with words that start with the same sound.

Left-to-right orientation This skill involves directionality. In English the direction is left to right. In Hebrew it is right to left, and in Chinese it is up and down. This skill can be developed by:

1 Using picture charts that go from left to right
2 Playing games that involve directionality
3 Hearing stories accompanied by pictures that are placed in sequence from left to right
4 Using pictures on a feltboard to tell stories

Visual memory This is the ability to recognize, reproduce, and recall accurately something that was seen before. It can be developed by:

1 Closing the eyes and describing what was seen
2 Imitating actions just seen
3 Recalling the details of an object or a group of objects

Motor coordination This refers to the control of the muscles and general body coordination. Motor coordination is necessary for the task of writing which lies ahead.

Children develop gross motor skills first. They need to be allowed to move, jump, climb, run, build, and use a hammer and saw. As the finer muscles develop, more detailed work is possible. We see changes in children's artwork; they string smaller beads, and they use the small muscles to do more delicate work.

Like all other areas of the curriculum, prereading skills grow out of experiences in the classroom that the children are interested in and enjoy. For example, suppose you find that a small group of children are interested in boats and water. Toy boats, stories about boats, and pictures of boats really involve them. They begin to develop the vocabulary for the various kinds of boats and bodies of water, such as lakes, oceans, streams, and puddles. Then they take a trip to an area where there are some boats. They learn additional vocabulary words. In talking to the people who work on the boats, they learn the names of the different parts of a boat, and they learn what is involved in sailing or

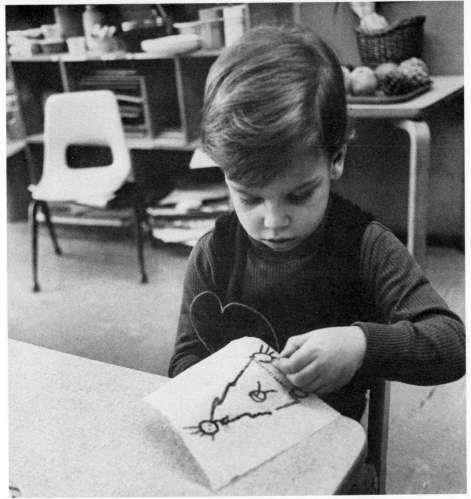

The child creates his own design and stitches it over, thus developing fine motor coordination.

fishing. When they return to the classroom, they excitedly recall and reconstruct the experience through discussions, dictated stories, and block building. They are involved in many prereading activities: the use of language, visual and auditory discrimination, left-to-right orientation, recall, and motor coordination. All these skills are being developed as part of an experience that is important to the children. These skills are not taught in abstract exercises. They become necessary prerequisites for communicating vital information to one another, to teachers, and to parents.

In playing with blocks, the child restructures his world. This helps him to conceptualize his experiences and provides an opportunity for discussion.

Activities for Reading Readiness

1 These are just a few of the many activities that aid in beginning reading:

Painting
Pasting
Cutting
Working puzzles
Working with clay
Pouring
Drawing
Weaving and sewing
Stringing beads
Hammering and sawing
Building with blocks

2 Guessing games are also helpful in beginning reading. Place several familiar objects in a bag and have the children guess what they are by touching and feeling them. Place familiar items such as cinnamon, garlic, and pepper in covered containers and have the children guess what they are by smelling them.

Activities for Auditory Discrimination

1 Have each child beat his or her name on a drum and compare the number of syllables with the number of syllables in another child's name:

Juan	Debbie	Roberto
Bob	Connie	Diana
Dot	Jimmy	Antoinette

2 Have the children clap to the rhythm of a song.

3 Have the children shut their eyes, listen to various sounds, try to guess what the sounds are. The sounds should be familiar ones, such as walking, stamping, clapping hands, sneezing, coughing, running, jingling money, opening a window, blowing a whistle, banging blocks, sweeping, splashing water, and cutting with scissors.

4 Hot Potato. Hide a familiar object in the room. One child closes his eyes and tries to find it. The other children clap their hands or sing a song loudly when the child is near the object and softly when he goes away from it.

5 Who Said That? One child closes his eyes, and another child says, "Hi, _____ [child's name]." The first child tries to guess who it was.

6 Point to objects in a book and ask the children to find things in the room that begin with the same beginning sound.

7 Say to the children, "If your name begins with the same sound as *dog*, sit down for snack." You could also say, "I'm looking for something in the room that starts like *candy* [clay]; we can roll it and pound it."

Activities for Visual Discrimination

1 You can have the children play color games, such as matching similar colors in a lotto game.

2 Say to the children, "I am looking at something in the room that is the color of Paul's shirt." The children name the color and find objects in the room that are of that color.

3 Take the children for a walk. When you return to school, have them dictate a list of the things they saw.

4 Place a few familiar objects on a table. One child shuts his eyes, and another child removes an object. The first child must try to guess which one was removed.

Activities for Classifying

Provide the children with a box of small objects or pictures of objects that go together, for example, a knife and a fork, a shoe and a sock, a hat and a coat, and a toothbrush and some toothpaste. Then have the children sort them according to their relationship.

Pictures of fruits and vegetables, zoo animals and farm animals, winter and summer clothing, etc., can also be offered for categorizing.

Reading Skills

Reading skills are presented to children only when they have had adequate preparation and show strength in all areas of reading readiness. The child's level of development is the most significant factor, not his or her age. Reading will probably not be part of the experience of most preschool children, but with an understanding and appreciation of the entire process, you will be able to help give the children in your class a solid foundation on which to build the basic reading skills that will follow.

Learning to read is a sequential process. It consists of these interrelated skills:

Word-recognition skills
Comprehension skills
Study skills

These three skill areas are interdependent. Formal reading can take place when all three skills are employed. Each of these skills has its own pattern of sequential development, proceeding from the simple to the complex. Let us explore each reading skill.

Word-recognition skills Let us use a cryptogram to establish the word-attack skills that are utilized to achieve word recognition:

%*-//-   *&%//*   *%// ///*
%*-//-   *&%//*   *-*:;*

You are equipped to break this code. You will be using all the word-attack skills that children use to achieve word recognition. Word recognition is completely dependent on the aforementioned prereading skills—visual and auditory discrimination, left-to-right progression, and life experiences that have resulted in language and knowledge. The word-attack skills you will have at your command include the use of:

1 Picture clues—using the accompanying picture to help identify a word shown with it
2 Configuration clues—recognizing a word because you remember its shape—for example, a long word containing double vowels and with tall letters extending above the line
3 Context clues—identifying a word by the words that surround it
4 Phonics—knowing the sounds that letters represent
5 Structural analysis—using known parts of words to identify new words

These word-attack skills, which make it possible for word recognition to take place, will now be explained in greater detail.

Picture and configuration clues   Look at Figure 6–1. Like the child, you slowly realize that the squiggles under the pictures are symbols for the word which identifies the picture. You recognize the picture as a representation of roses. You now designate the symbols of the word *roses*. You start to see each individual symbol in *roses*. As you become familiar with the symbols, you will find them in the cryptogram without the picture. When you learn the symbols, you will no longer need the picture.

You have now used two word-attack skills. You said the word by looking at the picture. This is called the "picture clue." You then recognized the word without the picture because you remembered the shape of the symbols, or the configuration. This is called the "configuration clue." Here is another example using both word-attack skills. As a child drinks a glass of milk, an adult directs the child's attention to the word *milk* on the container. Eventually, the child picks up the container, points to the word, and says "milk." If we show him the word *milk* printed on something other than a container, he evidences no recognition. In this situation, the container constitutes the picture. At present he says the word only in association with the picture, but someday he will see the word elsewhere and recognize it. "Look, that word is *milk*!" he exclaims proudly. This time he knows the word because he remembers its shape, or configuration.

Figure 6-1
Picture clues and configuration clues.

%*–//–

Children can learn many words by their configuration. They note tall and short letters, double vowels and consonants, and the length of the word. The teacher directs the children to look for clues. For instance, *see* is an easy word to identify. It has a squiggle and then a repeat. The "look and say" method, or sight method, relies very heavily on picture clues and configuration clues. A reasonable, careful selection of words that look different can be learned this way, but this method has its limitations. In order to progress in reading, other word-attack skills must be mastered. Now let us return to the cryptogram:

%*-//- &%// %// ///
%*-//- &%// -*:;

If you have used the clue to learn the configuration of *roses*, you can immediately find a repeat. Easy for you? Yes, but not so easy for an inexperienced child. Perhaps you have already confused // with ///. This will emphasize the need for visual-discrimination skills. Now that you are able to identify some letters in the cryptogram, you can transfer your knowledge to the symbols in the rest of the puzzle. You are still using the configuration. Placing all the letters you know, the cryptogram now reads:

ROSES &RE RE///

Context clues Because you know about roses, what you do now is use the surrounding symbols and your language, memory, information, and past experience to complete the first sentence of the learning problem:

ROSES ARE RED.

You didn't try to say *ire* or *ore*. You assumed *are* and then *red*. You used a context clue in your problem-solving situation. Reading the word *wind* is another example of the use of context clues. You cannot read this word and understand it unless you see it in a sentence; you need to know the meaning of the words that surround it—for example, "I *wind* the string into a ball" or "The *wind* is blowing." Applying the letters to the symbols you have already decoded, the second line of the cryptogram now looks like this:

ROSES ARE SO:;

Phonics We know the sound of *s* and *o*. Relying on the context and on the sound of these letters, you will finally solve the cryptogram with the word *soft*. If you did not know the sound of *s* and *o*, you might have said "Roses are nice" when you saw the second line of symbols. It was a combination of phonics and context which allowed you to identify the right word.

Phonics is the sounds that letters or groups of letters represent. Our alphabet consists of twenty-six letters, but the English language contains forty-four phonemes, or sounds. Phonics has to do with the various combinations, beginnings, endings, and groupings that make up the sound of our language. Here is another example of the use of context clues and phonics. Complete this: "The birthday c_____." The sound of *c* and the meaning of *birthday* have led you to the word *cake*. Without the phonic *c*, you might have said *party*.

Structural analysis   As we already stated, speech precedes reading. An understanding of structural analysis will alert teachers to the need for consciously involving themselves in language games that focus on parts of speech.

Structural analysis deals with parts of words. Some examples are:

Comparative endings. If a child knows *-er*, and *-est*, he has new words at his command: soft*er*, and soft*est*.

Tenses *-d*, *-ed*, *-ing*. When a child plays a game that results in speech patterns such as "I can jump," "I am jump*ing*," and "I jump*ed*," he again has new words at his command.

Compound words. *To* and *day* equal *today*, or *school* and *house* can become one word.

Possessives. -*'s*, and -*s'* (the dog's fur).

Contractions. *Don't*, and *what's*, for example.

The use of word-attack skills helped you to decode the cryptogram. As a result of their experience, very young children are constantly developing tools with which to solve learning problems. Through play they achieve sensory-motor development and visual and auditory discrimination, and they acquire language experiences on which to build more language and all the other prereading skills they need to attack a learning problem such as reading. Only when children have mastered reading-readiness skills can they advance to learning the use of the word-recognition skills that you employed, namely, picture clues, context clues, configuration clues, and phonics.

Comprehension skills   Now that you have solved the problems of word recognition and pronunciation, are you reading? Does recognizing a word or group of words constitute reading? Let's go one step further. Try reading this: *andingstronasstibale*. You can decode this "word" or translate the symbols into language through your knowledge of phonics. You can even say it. Are you reading? *No!* We call this "decoding." Reading is a skill process that must include word recognition and comprehension. Children must develop the understanding that written words have meaning and that a series of connected sentences are related to a single main thought.

Let us explore the comprehension skills. They are usually classified in three categories, and particular skills are required for competence in each one. They are:

1 Literal comprehension
2 Interpretive comprehension
3 Critical reading

Examine the use of these skills in the context of a brief story:

I know a little boy named José. When José went out to play, he watched the children roller skating. Oh, how José wanted skates! He would slide around and make believe he was skating. His mommy said he was still too little to have skates, so every day José looked at himself in the mirror. Then one snowy Christmas day his uncle gave him a present in a very heavy box. José opened the box. Guess what he found. A beautiful pair of roller skates. Many many days passed, and then at last all the snow was gone. Then José's uncle showed him how to fit the skates on his shoes. His uncle helped him skate on the sidewalk in front of his house. When he felt ready, his uncle stepped back and he skated on his own. As José skated away, his uncle called out, "Be careful."

Literal comprehension Literal questions that deal with the "who," "what," "when," and "where" could be: "What did José want?" "Who got them for him?" "When did he get them?" "Where did he skate?" Or a child could recall and retell the story. We are also concerned with a child's ability to recount a story in the correct sequence—to tell what happened first, second, etc. Does the child know who "he" is in the story? To what does "them" refer? Literal comprehension is the most elemental level of comprehension. Children often learn to respond to literal questions without ever being asked to evidence a further understanding of the material. It is vital that the teacher give the child a full opportunity to engage in a more profound level of comprehension. Literal comprehension alone does not indicate that a child really understands the material. He may be simply parroting responses.

Interpretive comprehension Interpretive comprehension indicates that a child sees a deeper meaning in the text even when it is not directly stated in the story. Can the child infer why José had to wait for the weather to change before he went skating, or why José kept looking in the mirror? Other questions can be asked to *assess* interpretive comprehension: "What happened to the snow?" (cause and effect). "How did José feel before and after he got the skates?" (comparing and contrasting emotions). "Why did José's uncle tell him to be careful?" (giving details not supplied in the story). "What kind of person do you think José's uncle was?" (identifying character, emotions, and motives). "What could happen next if José is not careful?" (predicting outcomes). "What could you call this story, or what is the *main idea* of the story?" These concepts help a child to develop language, and they allow the teacher to see whether the child has achieved this level of comprehension.

Critical reading Critical reading involves the highest form of comprehension. It must encompass literal and interpretive comprehension. Without these comprehension skills the child cannot read critically. The reader, or story listener, makes judgments about the story: "If José's mother felt he was too little, why did his uncle buy him skates?" "Why did his uncle buy him skates during the winter?"

As you read this book, you are engaged in critical reading. You check the accuracy of the statements, and you judge whether the various points are relevant. You try to determine what the authors' point of view is and what biases or prejudices they may have. Have emotionally charged words been used to sway your thinking? All this is critical reading.

These comprehension skills are indispensable, from the preschool years through adulthood. After the teacher reads a story to a child or a group of children, she must initiate questions in order to aid comprehension. It is important to ask literal, interpretive, and critical questions. Ever mindful of children's need to develop language skills, the teacher must word her questions so as to elicit language and not just "yes" or "no" responses. "How did José feel before and after he got the skates?" will elicit more language than, "Was José happy when he got the skates?"

Interpreting and evaluating must be encouraged in the prereading program. Encouraging children's thought processes by asking meaningful questions will eventually lead them to approach problems with natural curiosity. Many teachers ask very limited questions that elicit "yes" or "no" answers. There is also evidence that teachers focus on literal comprehension. Many children work puzzles with great facility and are never asked to use comprehension skills to interpret a picture. Children can "discover" who a person in a picture is when they are helped to notice a stethoscope or a drill or a television set and a repair kit. Children can look at a picture of a flower garden or of people wearing bathing suits or heavy coats and use these clues to interpret what season or kind of weather is being depicted. These experiences are vital parts of a reading program. As with word-recognition skills, teachers must realize that the foundation for comprehension skills is in the prereading program.

Study skills Having explored two basic reading skills—word recognition and comprehension—let us turn our attention to the third and last basic skill area: study skills. Study skills are used to read for a specific purpose. We read in order to make specific use of the content. We read to get specific information which we intend to use in a specific way. To do this successfully, we eventually need to learn how to select reading material and how to use a library, an index, a dictionary, and various reference sources. We then need to organize our facts and put them to use. It should be noted that comprehension skills are involved in study skills.

Like the other skills, study skills need to have roots in preschool experiences. The teacher can have the children select certain pictures from magazines—such as pictures of things with wheels or pictures of animals that live in water—and organize them in a specifically useful way. Nonreaders can develop a card file of recipes and then follow the directions on these cards when they cook. Pictures showing two cups and a container of milk, for example, will enable the children to "read" the cards and follow directions in an organized way, using two cups of milk for their recipe.

When a new pet arrives in the room, the teacher can read the children a book telling how to care for it.

The teacher can also have the children find the place in a storybook where a given incident happened. Preschool children locate information in books through the illustrations, but they are developing study skills.

Reading systems

There is a great deal of material on methods of teaching reading. All methods agree with the concept that reading is a process that must include word recognition, comprehension, and study skills; these three reading skills are the basis of all reading systems. Some methods focus on word recognition, and others on comprehension, while some approaches consider these skills to be inseparable.

Even in systems where the initial thrust is on word recognition, there are variations. Some methods focus on a sight vocabulary at the outset and then move to phonics. Sight-vocabulary methods are usually rooted in the belief that since learning goes from the known to the unknown, it is easier to begin by establishing "knowns" through a sight vocabulary, and then, using these familiar words, move on to phonics, the unknown. Some methods focus on phonics only, but the approaches to phonics differ greatly. A system may start with vowel sounds or consonant sounds. It may use pictures, objects, or colors to represent letter sounds. It may start with the initial or beginning sound of a word or with another part of the word. It may even develop letters representing the forty-four sounds in the English language. One approach focuses on the rhyming of words such as *sat*, *pat*, *fat*, and *rat*. All reading systems are related to the basic skills as stated.

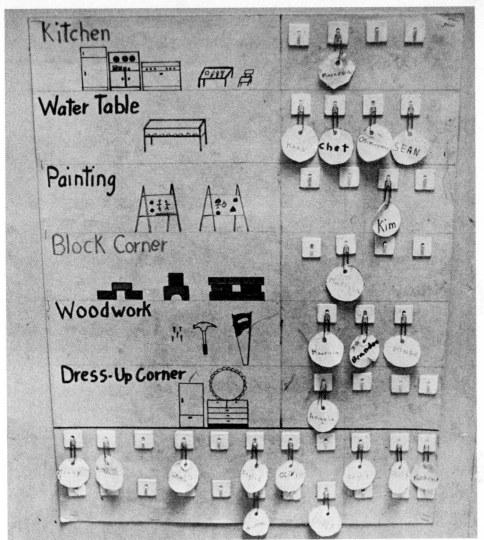

Job charts offer children experience with classification, help them to recognize symbols, and reinforce a positive self-concept.

The advantage of a highly structured formal reading program lies in its comprehensive nature. All the components of reading-skill development are clearly defined (requiring little knowledge on the part of the teacher). The system guides and dictates the nature of student involvement while sequential skills are developed. Teachers' dependence on such a fully explained system provides them with a feeling of security, which in turn generates a climate of security in the classroom.

There are individual children who thrive in a more structured situation, but there are a number of disadvantages inherent in the use of a highly structured system. To rely on any one system may mean that the social and emotional needs of some children are not met, and the uniqueness and individuality of each child may be minimized. If we assume that children should be encouraged to develop their creativity and independence and that this is vital in order to enable them to be self-activators in the future, then these structured systems are sorely lacking.

Whatever the reading system or its emphasis, the teacher's concern should be the value of the program in relation to the children for whom it is designed. Teachers need to adapt systems and methods to children, not children to methods and systems. The literature suggests that each individual is different with respect to genetic endowment, temperament, and predisposition. The methods that teachers design must take those individual differences into account. Each child has the right to have every opportunity to achieve his or her potential.

Teachers must ask themselves whether any one method could possibly be effective for all children. We all have different nutritional needs, sleep needs, recreational needs, and emotional needs. We also have different learning needs. Each child comes to the classroom with positive and negative experiences that have contributed to the formation of his individual personality. He has certain very definite interests and character traits. No matter how hard the teacher tries to categorize or classify him, he remains unique. Once the teacher understands the process of teaching reading, it must be adapted to the individual child. It is appropriate and necessary for the teacher to ask, "How can I engage the interests of individual children in a large class and create a climate for learning?"

Many teachers have begun to use techniques developed in the individualized reading approaches and to conduct individual conferences with each child while the rest of the class is working and playing. During the individual discussion, the teacher tries to determine each child's strengths, weaknesses, and specific learning needs and learning style. No system is effective without the teacher's full knowledge of the sequential levels of learning.

In teaching reading, it is essential for the professional to be completely familiar with all aspects of the reading program. But for a reading program to be successful, it is equally important that the teacher understand children's developmental needs and the needs of our society as a whole.

Reading-Skill Games

1 Play a song on the record player or play an instrument and invite the children to move in any way they wish. You can then hold up cards

showing action pictures or words (*run*, *jump*, *skip*, *turn around*) and tell the children to move the way the words or pictures say to. This game can be presented to the children after they have had many experiences moving to music.

2 Alphabet Bingo. This game is played with four or five children. Each bingo card should contain fifteen capital letters. Make several individual cards of each letter. The children match the letters called to the letters on their cards. The first child to fill all of one column or one row wins the game and must call out all the letters in the winning column or row.

There are many variations of this game. You can use lowercase letters only, a combination of lowercase letters and capital letters, numbers, items that go together (socks and shoes or salt and pepper, for example) rhyming words, the children's names, new reading words, etc.

3 Go Fish. Use 3- by 5-inch index cards. Make two cards for each letter (capital or lowercase) in the alphabet, two cards for the name of each child in the room, or two cards for each of about twenty-five familiar reading words. Four children can play. Each child receives five cards. The remaining cards are the fishpond. If a child has two of a kind, he puts them aside. To start the game, one child asks the child to his right whether he has any "Johns." If he doesn't, the child is told to "go fish." If he picks a "John," he goes again. The game ends when the fishpond is empty; the child with the most pairs wins.

4 Letter cubes (for studying word families). You can purchase a letter-cube game, but it's a lot cheaper to make one. Thread four small square beads on a pipe cleaner. Knot the pipe cleaner at each end. Write individual letters on sticky peel-off tape and stick the letters on the exposed sides of the beads. The child turns the beads to make many different words. (This idea can also be used for learning mathematical concepts. Numbers can be substituted for letters, and plus, minus, and equals signs can be added.) Small square blocks can also be used, but you will need an electric drill to make the holes.

5 Sentence puzzles. Write a sentence on a piece of sturdy cardboard and then cut the sentence into a puzzle. The puzzle pieces can be put in a box or envelope and then given to a child to assemble.

6 The words of new songs can be posted on the walls for sight reading. Jump-rope songs, rhymes, and chants are popular. Leave room for additional rhymes or chants.

7 Provide class books of rhymes, puzzles, etc., leaving space so that the children can add to them. Books of photographs of the children, with dictated stories accompanying the pictures, are favorites.

Reading Stories

Children love stories and poems. Even before they have started to speak, young children become absorbed in looking at pictures of things familiar to them. They need an adult who enjoys sharing pictures and picture books with them. Research has repeatedly demonstrated that children who hear stories develop language more readily. Children who hear stories have less difficulty in learning how to read.

Content Children become wide-eyed with excitement when we tell them stories about themselves. "When you were a baby you loved to. . . ." Repetition doesn't make this boring. Preschool children are learning about their world and all the people in it. Make-believe can take place only when the child has some understandings of the reality on which it is based. The child can make believe she is "Mommy" because she has a knowledge of the role of a mother.

Children enjoy stories about the familiar—families, children, infants, vehicles, toys, schools, colds, and feelings of anger, pain, jealousy, frustration, and joy. Stories dealing with greed, revenge, or the desire for power, which are common themes in fairy tales, are more appropriate for older children, who have had more experiences and can therefore understand more complicated emotions. Some books also deal successfully with numbers, shapes, scientific concepts, and material from other curriculum areas. Children usually dislike books that moralize.

Illustrations Children enjoy pictures that are understandable; they do not necessarily have to be realistic. A highly stylized, simplified illustration is appropriate if it is easily identified by the child. Colors don't have to be realistic. A child's book needs to have pictures that relate to the story line. A picture and the incident it illustrates are usually on facing pages.

Style Short sentences and simple language capture children's attention. Repeated catch phrases, rhythmical repeats, nonsense words, and rhymes are also very useful and enjoyable. Children's stories need to have one simple idea which is developed into a single plot. Children find it confusing to listen to a story that has several plots or too many characters. Children enjoy being able to anticipate the story's development, but they also like occasional surprises. Children's language development is enhanced even more by the inclusion of rich and sensitive descriptions, which appear in many children's books.

Children appreciate humor, but only if it relates to what they understand. Children must first understand roles and functions before they can see any humor in a distortion of them.

In order to enjoy Ruth Krauss' book *Backward Day*,* children need to understand the sequence of events in their daily lives; otherwise, they will not see the humor in putting on shoes before socks and then going down the stairs backwards and sitting backwards to eat.

---

*Ruth Krauss, *The Backward Day*, Harper & Row, New York, 1950.

In Marjorie Flack's book *Angus and the Cat*,* we see Angus, the dog, looking out a dormer window. He can't find the cat, who is sitting calmly next to the dormer. If children understand the structure of the roof as shown in the picture, they will laugh because they realize that they can see the cat but Angus can't.

Format Books should be sturdy. Pop-up pictures quickly tear in young hands. A binding that is well stitched and allows the book to open flat without breaking will last longer and give greater satisfaction to children as they "read" to themselves. Heavy paper allows children to turn pages without tearing them.

Before you read You should be familiar with the story. It is not necessary to memorize it, but you should understand the main idea. *Snowy Day*, by Ezra Keats,‡ is about a boy, Peter, who does many things in the snow. He builds a snowman, he makes footprints in the snow, etc. After playing, he puts a snowball in his pocket and goes home. When his mother helps undress him for his bath, he is very perplexed because his socks are wet. During his bath he keeps wondering about those wet socks. As soon as his bath is over, he goes to check the snowball in his pocket and finds it gone. He goes to sleep and dreams of more snow. When he wakes up he finds that the snow is still there. The concept that is important in this story is not just snow, but the melting of snow, as implied by the wet socks and the snowball.

Story time starts with a short discussion with the children. This discussion draws on the children's own experiences with snow. Any unfamiliar word that appears in the story can be introduced during the discussion. This encourages the children to use language and leads into the story. The teacher then picks up the book and says something like, "I have a story here about a little boy who played in the snow, just as you did. The name of the book is *Snowy Day*. It was written by Ezra Keats." Introducing books helps the children to learn that books, like people, have names. It also helps them see that someone writes books.

Telling the story When you read a book to a group of children, sit facing them at their own eye level. Hold the book so that the children can see the pages. If you hold your thumb behind the book and put your other four fingers in front of it, you have the freedom to move the book so that all the children can see the pictures. The book is held open in this position in front of your shoulder. This allows you to see the printed material and at the same time maintain eye contact with the group.

The current generation of children, accustomed to watching television actors, responds well to a reader who can use her voice dramatical-

---

*Marjorie Flack, *Angus and the Cat*, Doubleday, Garden City, N.Y., 1931.
‡Ezra Jack Keats, *Snowy Day*, Viking, New York, 1962.

A comfortable place, a properly held book, an interesting story, an expressive reading—
and see how interested the children are.

ly. Voice changes representing different characters, animals, and
sounds are a further help in holding children's interest. The reading is
enhanced if you change the pace of your reading to correspond to the
action of the story. Pauses facilitate participation. A slight pause before
an obvious word, name, or refrain often stimulates the children to supply
it.

Children sometimes interrupt a story with a comment or a question.
How to handle this often puzzles teachers. It is impossible to blueprint
an answer, but here are some things to think about:

1   The interruption may be more valuable than the story. Perhaps it
will serve to encourage the group to use language. In that case, the book
can wait.

2   It may be possible to handle the interruption with a brief assuring
comment and then proceed with the reading.

3   The interruption might be a deliberate attempt to interfere with
the group's enjoyment. You can judge this if you know the child. If this is
the case, you can try to help him wait until the end of the story.

4 A child might be upset by something in the story. Knowing the child, you meet his needs. He may want to sit on your lap or hold your hand, for example.

You should not repeatedly interrupt your reading to explain or interpret what you are reading. If the book is appropriate for the group, it will speak for itself. If it contains many unfamiliar words and long, complicated thoughts, you should not be reading it or should substitute other phrases.

After the reading   Children often like to discuss a story after they have heard it. In this discussion, you should seek to discover the children's comprehension ability. All comprehension skills can be developed at this time (see the section on reading-comprehension skills). The literal questions of "who," "what," "when," and "where" are not sufficient. You need to deal with interpretation and critical skills as well. "Why did Peter worry about his wet socks?" Did the children realize that Peter was in the snow, not in water? "How, then, did his socks get wet?" "Why did the wet socks make him check the snowball in his pocket?" In this discussion, language skills are also developed. It is extremely important to word questions in a way that elicits language. Avoid questions that can be answered with a "yes" or a "no."

Sometimes a story may lend itself to dramatic reenactment after the children are familiar with it. You simply help them decide which characters they would like to be. Provide appropriate props and then let the children play out the story in their own way, using their own language. This is best accomplished without adult interference.

Children love hearing some books over and over again; knowing what is going to happen gives them a sense of security and power. After a book has been read, it should be placed within easy reach of the children. Given the proper environment, they will read it to themselves and to their friends.

You should try to read at least one story every day. It is important to understand that an entire class is not necessarily interested in the same book or ready to hear a story at the same time. You might begin reading a story to four children. As you continue to read, children may drift in and out of the group. You may end up with fifteen children or five children. Respect for individual differences and needs makes this acceptable.

Enjoy reading stories. It is fun. Children usually enjoy what we enjoy if we communicate our pleasure.

MATHEMATICS

In our daily lives we are constantly using mathematics or mathematical concepts. Mathematics is useful, it is practical, and it helps us order our experiences. Mathematics is not a set of abstract, meaningless formulas, but a method that people have developed to deal with the world around them. Mathematics grew out of people's need to master their environment. When we find a page in a book, when we measure things for cooking or building, and when we pay for groceries or tell time, we are relying on mathematical skills we have learned. Mathematics is also part of children's lives. Teachers need to point out the mathematical experiences that occur in children's lives and bring the learning to the conscious and verbal level. An approach to mathematics that flows from the children's experiences and interests can result in a positive attitude and will provide practice in logical thinking and problem solving.

Like all curriculum areas, mathematics is not an isolated activity, but is an integral part of the entire program.

Every area in the room presents opportunities for mathematical learning. For example:

> *In the housekeeping area*
> Are there enough pegs on the pegboard to hang up all the coats?
> Do we have enough forks for everyone to eat dinner?
> *In the block area*
> How many unit blocks does it take to make a double unit?
> Put all the triangles on the top.
> Does that block have a curved or a straight edge?
> *In the manipulative-toy area*
> How many red cubes are there?
> Can you find the puzzle piece that fits here?
> How many wheels are there on the car?
> *In the woodworking area*
> Is this nail long enough to hold these two pieces of wood together?
> We need a thicker piece of wood.
> *In the water-play area*
> How many cups of water will it take to fill up this container?

Everyday Materials Can Be Mathematical Materials

Stones found in the yard lend themselves to many activities in mathematics. They can be:

Ordered. Place some stones in order of size, color, or shape—from small to large, from light to dark, from flat to round, or from thin to fat.

Counted. Arrange some stones into sets by color, size, etc. (count the sets and subsets).

Weighed. Compare (on a scale) rocks with stones, stones with sand, etc.

Estimated. Ask the children how many stones are needed to fill a container.

Figure 6-2
A classroom table can be measured in pencil lengths.

Measured. Compare a line of five small stones with a line of five big stones, etc. Furniture in the room can be measured in a variety of ways. For example, ask the children how many pencils make up the length of a table (Figure 6-2). Try using different parts of the body, such as fingers, hands, or feet, to measure the length of the table.

Everyday Experiences Can Be Applied to Mathematics

At snack time, each child takes two carrots. Apples are cut into four pieces. Ask a child how many seeds she found in her piece of watermelon.

At lunch, each child gets one fork, one spoon, and one plate.

Measure children at the beginning of the year and at the end of the year and have them discuss the differences.

Baking cookies includes measuring, counting, and possibly making shapes.

The water table provides opportunities to explore the concepts of empty, full, heavy, and light, for example.

The children can also make a chart that records the different amounts of water which different containers hold. Figure 6-3 is an example.

Figure 6-3
Measure the capacity of various containers.

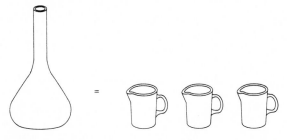

Mathematics Is a Way to Order and Structure the World

Mathematics deals with:

Size
Shape
Amount
Space
Time

It means:

Putting things in groups and comparing these groups
Measuring and comparing the volume, weight, length, and area of things in time and space

In order to develop these skills, the teacher creates an environment that will enable the children to make discoveries. There are three steps that children must pass through in mathematical learning.

1 Free experimentation Providing a variety of materials allows the children to see how the materials feel and to discover what can be done with them. They see that water pours, that blocks stack, that puzzle shapes fit, that things are too small or too large, etc. They learn that materials are either "continuous," like sand and water, or "discontinuous," like blocks, beads, and other things that can be separated into pieces or units.

2 Introduction of vocabulary The teacher encourages the use of words like *same/different, full/empty, more/less, whole/part.*

3 Emergence of problems Questions arise from conversations during play. For example, the children ask, "Which weighs more, the book or the pencil?" "Does water make sand heavier?" "How many more blocks are needed to complete the bridge?" The problems come from the children's experience, and so they are motivated to seek solutions.

In the early childhood curriculum, mathematics includes:

Number skills
Measurement
Geometry

Number Skills

1 Using number names. For things like ages, room numbers, and addresses. Also used in stories.

2 One-to-one correspondence. Matching buttons to buttonholes, coats to hats, straws to a milk container, shoes to feet, three beds to three bears, etc.

3 Perceiving the number of objects in a set and its subsets without counting. A set of three cups may contain two green cups and one red cup. The child perceives the number of grouped cups without counting. It is believed that children can conceptualize a number that is their age.

4 Conserving number. Rearranging a set but still having the same quantity. One red cup and two green cups equal the same quantity as two green cups and one red cup.

5 Understanding the empty set. If we have five cookies and six plates and we put one cookie on each plate, we will have one empty set, or one empty plate.

6 Comparing sets. Seeing which sets are the same and which are different in terms of number. Using words like *equal*, *more*, and *less* and eventually using symbols, such as an equal sign (=). Each set has one straw, one milk container, and one cookie. They are equal sets.

7 Ordering sets. Putting sets in order from those with the least to those with the most number of things.

8 Rote counting. This is counting in order—one, two, three, etc. It can be taught through songs or rhythmic repetition.

9 Recognizing written or printed numerals. Reading "1" and "one" as the same thing.

10 Associating number and numeral. Matching sets of objects to a symbol, such as a set of three things to a 3.

11 Matching cardinal numbers (one, two, three) to ordinal numbers (first, second, third). Seeing a set within an ordered series. Using 1st, 2d; first, second; etc.

12 Forming the union of sets. Determining the number of objects in the set when two or more sets have been added together. Eventually using the symbol for "plus" (+).

13 Subtracting sets. Determining how many are left when one set is taken away from another. Eventually using the symbol for "minus" (−).

14 Using the number line. Developing the concept of a number of things in a line from bottom to top, front to back, and left to right. Putting numerals in order from left to right.

Measurement

1 Linear measurement. Discriminating longer and shorter, ordering lengths, etc. Using one object as a standard measure. Introducing standard units of measure, such as inches and feet. Using a straight-edge, a ruler, etc.

2 Liquid measurement. Exploring and comparing different quantities

of liquid. Using one container as a standard measure. Introducing cup, pint, etc.

3 Currency measurement. Recognizing and naming each coin. Discriminating one coin from another and learning the value of each. Older children also will be ordering, combining, and exchanging currency.

Geometry

1 Plane geometry. Recognizing, naming, and comparing basic shapes such as the circle, square, triangle, and rectangle. These shapes are found in blocks, toys, cookies, windows, floor tiles, and many other things that are part of the children's everyday lives.

2 Solid geometry. Becoming familiar with shapes such as spheres, cones, cylinders, and cubes by handling everyday objects like balls, blocks, cans, cups, and foods. A banana is cylindrical; if we slice it, we get disks.

Mathematical Learning Can Be Very Personal

Children's own experiences contain a wealth of potential applications to mathematics. There is much about children that lends itself to mathematical activities. Children love to match, compare, and measure their fingers, toes, ears, hands, legs, and arms. They love to compare their height with the height of others. They learn that some people are shorter, and others taller; they learn that they are like other people in some ways

Figure 6-4

Charting children's birthdays. Other things can be similarly charted, such as pets ("cat," "dog," "bird," "gerbil," and so on as the column heads) or number of siblings or number of windows in bedroom ("1," "2," "3," "4," etc. as column heads).

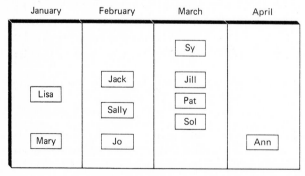

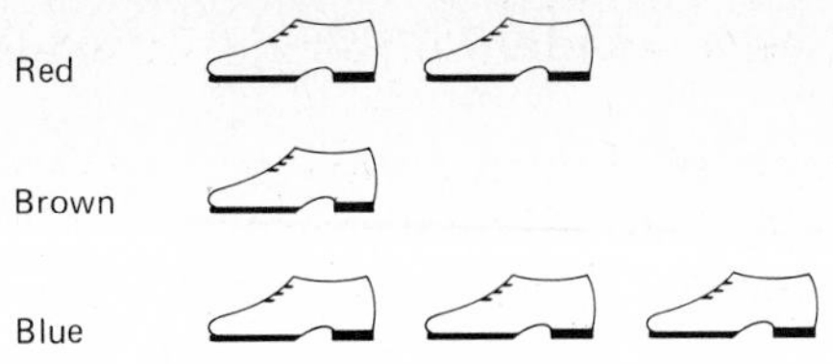

Red

Brown

Blue

	Black	Red	Brown	Leather
Joe	x			x
Alice		x		
Mark				x
Annie			x	x

Figure 6-5
Charting children's shoes.

and different from them in other ways. Learning such things satisfied children's sense of self and helps them find out about others.

This kind of personal application of mathematics, like a variety of mathematical concepts, can be recorded with a graph. Figure 6-4 shows how children can chart their birthdays. Each child has a piece of paper with his or her name on it, which he pastes in the proper column. The child can look at a graph like this and see results. He can also refer back to this information when he wants to. Figure 6-5 shows another type of graph for personal applications of mathematics.

Note the many similarities between mathematics and the other curriculum areas. They all use problem-solving techniques, and they all use the senses; in all of them, children must be active participants in the learning. This active experience enables them to deal confidently with real problems that emerge. They are then interested in the solutions. We call this "learning through *discovery*."

Mathematical Vocabulary

There are a great many mathematical terms that children need to use and understand. These words can be introduced in a variety of settings and in many kinds of activities. For instance, the teacher can point out that beginning and ends are used in stories and that a cup and a teaspoon are part of a recipe.

The age of the child will influence which of the following words are most appropriate and useful.

Size Big, bigger than, biggest, little, small, smaller than, smallest, large, larger than, largest, long, longer than, longest, short, shorter than, shortest, tall, taller than, tallest, high, higher than, highest, low, lower than, lowest, wide, wider than, widest, fat, fatter than, fattest, narrow, more narrow, narrowest, thin, thinner than, thinnest, deep, deeper than, deepest, broad, broader than, broadest, great, greater than, greatest, light, lighter than, lightest, heavy, heavier than, heaviest, thick, thicker than, thickest.

Amount Few, fewer than, fewest, more, more than, most, less, less than, least, how many, how much, how often, how fast, how long, how slow, in all, enough, as much as, none, some, many, all, several, any, couple, pair, group, bunch, amount, ton, pint, quart, cup, teaspoon, tablespoon, gallon, half gallon, drop, degree, handful, spoonful, cupful, a pinch of, part, entire, whole, carton, case, tankful, a little bit, peck, bushel, each, every, only, full, empty, single, double, almost.

Placement Top, bottom, middle, first, last, second, third, fourth, fifth, sixth, seventh, eighth, ninth, tenth, next, near, nearer than, nearest, far, farther than, farthest, close, closer than, closest, here, there, left, right, up, down, before, after, around, inside, outside, under, over, below, beneath, beside, between, across, behind, past, above, toward, from, to, away from, on, off, upon, into, with, throughout.

Time Beginning, end, later, not now, in a little while, after awhile, a little longer, day, noon, midnight, morning, afternoon, evening, today, tomorrow, yesterday, month, last month, next month, week, next week, last week, year, next year, last year, calendar, season, date, number of hours in a day, number of minutes in an hour, quarter till the hour, names of the days of the week, names of the months of the year, number of days in a week, number of weeks in a year, number of days in a year, number of months in a year, winter, spring, summer, fall, autumn, sunrise, time to eat, time to rest, o'clock, annually, daily, weekly, hourly, monthly, yearly, soon, when.

Shape Round, square, circle, triangle, rectangle, straight, curved.

Measurement Foot, feet, inch, yard, pound, ounce, dozen, half dozen, scale, ruler, yardstick, mile, half mile, peck, bushel, height, weight, length; metric units.

Processes Either, or, neither, nor, equal, and, are, too, get, altogether, together, put together, add, take away.

Making Mathematical Games for Children

Patterning Use cubes or blocks to build patterns that the children can imitate (Figure 6-6). Make a drawing of the pattern that the children can duplicate with cubes or blocks.

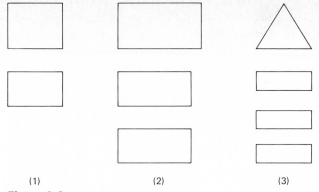

(1)   (2)   (3)

Figure 6-6
Block patterns.

Matching sets   Make a lotto game with matching sets of objects (Figure 6-7).

   On a piece of posterboard, draw two rows of boxes. Put different numbers of dots in the boxes in one row, and attach cups in the boxes in the other row. The children put the appropriate number of objects (buttons or pebbles, for example) in the different cups. They can check themselves by matching the number of objects in each cup to the number of dots directly above it (Figure 6-8). You could add another row giving numerals directly above the dots.

Figure 6-7
Lotto with pictures.

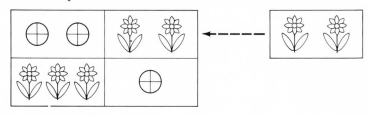

Figure 6-8
Matching sets.

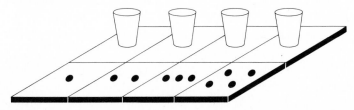

Figure 6-9
Jigsaw-puzzle number.

Figure 6-10
Matching numerals and numbers.

Learning to recognize numerals   Make numerals from cardboard and trace them on sandpaper. Cut out the sandpaper numerals and paste them to the cardboard ones. Let the children "feel" the shapes of the numerals with their fingers.

Make large numerals from cardboard. Cut them into puzzles for the children to fit together (Figure 6-9). Note: Use paper colored on one side only, so that the children won't put the puzzles together backward. Keep each puzzle in a separate envelope.

Make a bingo game using the numerals 1 to 10, but randomly place only nine on a card so that each one is different.

Associating numerals with numbers   Make numerals out of cardboard. The children then put the appropriate number of disks on each numeral (Figure 6-10). For younger children, put the number of dots on each numeral—the children then match the disks to the dots.

Make a fishing pole, using a magnet as a hook. Cut fish from construction paper. Put a different number of dots on each fish and place a paper clip on each. The children "catch" a fish, count the dots on it, and then put it in the box with that number on it (Figure 6-11).

Make cards with a different numeral on each. Staple down one side of a rectangle on each card to make a "door." The children try to recognize the numeral. Then they open the door to see if they are right. The correct number of dots is shown inside the door (Figure 6-12). This same setup can also be used for addition, with the answer inside the door.

Figure 6-11
Fishing game for associating numerals and numbers.

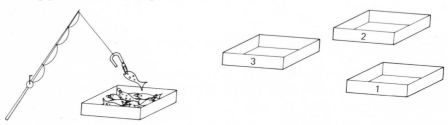

Figure 6-12
Open the door to find the answer.

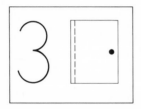 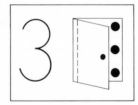

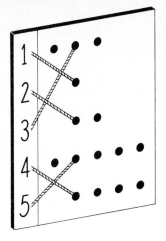

Figure 6-13
Numerals and dots must be
connected correctly.

Make a chart on posterboard. On one side write numerals and on the other side put the corresponding numbers of dots, but not directly opposite the appropriate numerals. Attach pieces of string or yarn to the side with the numerals (Figure 6-13). The children use the string or yarn to connect the numerals to the appropriate rows of dots. The same idea can be used for matching numerals to number games and for matching sets of objects with the appropriate number.

Ordering sets Cut a long strip of posterboard and put different sets of dots along the strip. Cut the strip so that the sets interlock only in the correct order (Figure 6-14). Note: The pieces interlock with the same number of bumps as dots. This idea can also be used to order numerals.

Addition Cut strips of paper and fold them one-third over. Draw dots on the outside of the folded piece and some more on the rest on the strip to the right of the folded piece. On the inside of the folded piece, write the numeral indicating the total number of dots (Figure 6-15). This can also be done in reverse, with all the dots inside (Figure 6-16), so that the children must figure out how many more dots are needed to make the number indicated by the numeral.

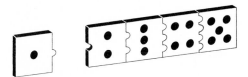

Figure 6-14
Putting sets in order.

Folded: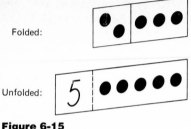

Unfolded: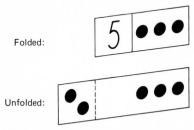

Figure 6-15
Addition.

Folded:

Unfolded:

Figure 6-16
Subtraction.

Finger Plays That Use Mathematical Concepts

TWO LITTLE HUMMINGBIRDS   TWO TO FIVE YEARS
(Your thumbs are the birds.)
Two little hummingbirds sitting on a hill,
One named Jack, the other named Jill.
Fly away, Jack.
Fly away, Jill.
No little hummingbirds sitting on a hill.
Come back, Jack.
Come back, Jill.
Two little hummingbirds sitting on a hill.

A BALL   TWO TO FIVE YEARS
(Use your hands to show different sizes of balls, from small to large.)
Here is a ball,
And here is a ball.
And a great big ball I see.
Shall we count them?
One, two, three.

THE BEEHIVE

(Make a fist with your hand. This is the beehive. Put out a finger as you count each bee. Begin with your thumb.)

Here is the beehive. Where are the bees?
Hidden away where nobody sees.
Soon they come creeping out of the hive.
One! Two! Three! Four! Five!

BEAT ONE HAMMER   FOUR AND FIVE YEARS

My mother told me to tell you
To beat one hammer   *(Pound one fist.)*
Like you see me do.
My mother told me to tell you
To beat two hammers   *(Pound two fists.)*
Like you see me do.
My mother told me to tell you
To beat three hammers   *(Pound two fists;*
Like you see me do.   *stamp one foot.)*
My mother told me to tell you
To beat four hammers   *(Pound two fists;*
Like you see me do.   *stamp two feet.)*
My mother told me to tell you
To beat five hammers   *(Add nodding head.)*
Like you see me do.
My mother told me to tell you
To beat no hammers   *(Stop!)*
Like you see me do.

ONE, TWO TIE MY SHOE   TWO TO FIVE YEARS
(Actions accompany the words.)

One, two, tie my shoe.
Three, four, shut the door.
Five, six, pick up sticks.
Seven, eight, shut the gate.
Nine, ten, a big fat hen.

TEN IN THE BED   FOUR AND FIVE YEARS
(Can be played with just five fingers.)

There were ten in the bed,   *(Hold up 10 fingers.)*
And the little one said,
"Roll over, roll over."   *(Roll hands one over the other.)*
So they all rolled over,   *(Hold up 10 fingers; then put down*
And one fell out,   *one finger, leaving nine up.)*
And then there were nine.
(Repeat the song again and again, each time putting one more finger down.
When there are only two left, sing the following lines.)
There were two in the bed,   *(Hold up two fingers)*
And the little one said,
"Roll over, roll over."   *(Roll hands one over the other.)*
So they all rolled over,   *(Hold up two fingers; put one down.)*
And one fell out,

And then there was one.
And the little one said,   *(Move little finger.)*
"Good Night!"

SCIENCE: AN ATTITUDE AND A METHOD

Science is a part of the early childhood curriculum that can help children have a better feeling about themselves by giving them an understanding of the world around them. The curious child will naturally ask questions about the things he or she observes:

> Do ants have eyes?
> Do flowers eat?
> Where did the day go?
> Where was I before I was born?

These questions are typical of children's attempts to understand their new experiences in the light of what they already know. They can be the basis for far-reaching scientific explorations and journeys to discovery—if we are willing to go with the child.

Children's questions about the natural and physical world may amuse us and may stimulate our thinking, but they often trigger off some uneasy feelings too. They remind us that there are many things that we still don't understand. Our own confusion can help us sympathize with the child's desire to give the world some order, or it can frighten us. Some teachers back off from all areas of science because of this fear. They may also avoid science because of their own experiences in science courses when they were students.

Our Own Feelings about Science

What do you think of when the word *science* is mentioned? Does it conjure up images of test tubes and formulas? Many people picture the scientist as someone who is buried in a laboratory or locked in a room with a computer or some other strange machine. The world of the scientist seems just about as far from the early childhood classroom as one can get.

Science isn't part of early school memories for most of us. Those days were for "reading, 'riting, and 'rithmetic," with just a little time left over for art or music. Science was something we remember from high school. It appeared suddenly as a separate and (for the majority of us) troublesome subject. Many people associate science with a course in chemistry or physics which was complicated, difficult, or just plain impossible.

Since much of their experience with science seems remote and irrelevant, teachers may find it hard to see how it can be an exciting part of the early childhood curriculum. Yet science is by no means irrelevant. On the contrary, it is very basic. It is part of everything and exists around us everywhere. While science may have made you feel overwhelmed, it *can* help you, and the children with whom you work, make sense out of things. Instead of making you feel inadequate, it can help give you greater confidence in dealing with the things in your environment.

Science Is a Daily Experience

Children come to school possessing a wealth of information that can be developed into scientific investigations. They can now do things they couldn't do when they were babies. They experience a change in the weather by the different clothes they wear. They may have noticed how a tree near their house is different at different times of the year. Many have ridden bicycles and know the sensation of pedaling fast down a hill,

The teacher's interest is communicated to the child as he explores the possibilities in batteries and bulbs.

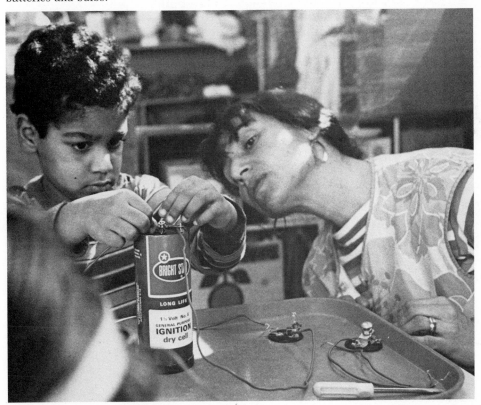

and they also know the effort it takes to get back up that same hill. Many have felt snow melt in the bottom of their pockets or have splashed through puddles after a heavy rain. Science can be a way to help children gain a greater understanding of these varied experiences.

The science curriculum grows out of the children's everyday life experiences. At home, children watch dinner being prepared and see the changes that take place when something is heated or cooked. They turn on the television set or the lights, and they see appliances being plugged into the wall. If there are plants at home, they may have noticed that they are kept where there is the most light. Discussions can develop about the things the children have seen at home and can provide similar experiences in the classroom to determine what the children understand or misunderstand about these things. Additional experiences can then be planned to correct or broaden the children's knowledge. For instance, the children can attach a small bulb to a battery and turn it on and off with a switch. After a discussion about what plants need to grow, the children can experiment with putting different plants in different parts of the classroom to see where they will grow best—in the window, in the closet, or someplace in the center of the room. They can also observe how plants grow toward the light; the children can mark one side of a flower pot, turn it around, and see how the plant begins to grow the other way.

There are many other materials and activities in the classroom that stimulate science learning. A small group of children playing with blocks may have noticed how a car goes much faster down a ramp than along the ground. They may also try to see what happens if the incline of the ramp is increased. There are opportunities for scientific experiences in many different parts of the room and at many different times during the day.

Housekeeping area   Making play dough provides an opportunity to feel the different textures of flour and salt and watch them change when they are mixed with water.

Art area   Mixing different colors of paint is an experiment that children enjoy. Using clay and seeing it change when water is added to it or when it is left out on the radiator can also lead to discoveries.

Music area   Experiments in the nature of sound can include filling containers of the same size with different-sized beans and then shaking them; tapping on glasses containing different amounts of water; and watching different-sized rubber bands vibrate on a cigar box.

Woodworking area   Pounding nails into different kinds of wood will lead to some interesting scientific observations. For example, nails go into some woods more easily than into others.

Block area   Making a tower of blocks or a building that doesn't fall and loading up a truck with heavy blocks are experiences that help the children learn about the physical properties of materials.

During snack time Observing the different kinds of seeds in apples, pears, grapefruits, etc., can lead to an experiment in growing different kinds of plants.

Outdoors Collecting leaves can help the children observe the variety in nature and can stimulate sorting, matching, and classifying activities.

There may also be a separate science area in the room. Here the children might care for a guinea pig or a gerbil; they might set up their collection of leaves, shells, or stones; or they could experiment to see whether a magnet will attract various objects that the teacher has set out on a table.

A Scientific Study

There are daily occurrences that can be turned into extensive scientific studies. One such activity is playing with sand. Look at a group of children in the sandbox.

First with dry sand What do the children do with the dry sand? They will probably run their fingers through it. Without saying a word, they are finding out how it feels. They may try various ways of picking it up. After the children have explored the sand by themselves, you can ask questions and help them verbalize these sensory experiences and discoveries. For example, you can ask, "What happens if you cup your hands and try to lift the sand?" "What happens if you open your fingers?"

Then with dry sand and added materials You can then introduce scoops, shovels, and containers to stimulate new discoveries. The children will probably try filling up one of the containers with sand. You can ask, "Which tool picks up more sand, the shovel or the scoop?" Using shovels and scoops of different sizes can make this stage of discovery more fascinating. A sieve presents new problems. You might ask, "Why doesn't the sieve pick up the sand?" "If there were some pebbles in the sand, would they fall through the sieve too?"

Then with wet sand Adding water to the sand creates another exciting dimension. Some questions here might be: "How does the water change the sand?" "What can you do with wet sand that you couldn't do with dry sand?" "How long does it take to dry the sand in a shady corner of the room? In the sun? On the radiator?"

As you listen and watch the children, you will get many clues for new avenues of investigation. You can also present some new ideas to see whether they arouse the children's curiosity.

Depending on the resources available in your community, the children may be able to find answers to such questions as:

Where do we find sand?
What animals live in or near sand?
What plants grow in sand?
How are plants, animals, water, and sand interrelated?

Areas of Study

Sand is just one material that can lead to a scientific investigation; the science curriculum in the early childhood program can cover a wide range of topics. These can be divided into the biological and physical sciences, which can be further divided into other content areas such as the following.

Living things   The study of plants and animals and what they need to survive and reproduce.

Matter and energy   The study of electricity, magnetism, light, and sound.

The earth and its resources   The study of rocks, water, air, weather, and the seasons.

The earth and space   The study of the sun, the moon, and the planets, as well as the study of astronauts and space. While this is clearly the most abstract area, today's children are fascinated with some aspects of this topic.

Scientific Concepts

Certain concepts run through all aspects of science. They are connecting links between various areas of study, and the teacher can draw attention to them whenever they come up. Some of these concepts are:

Change   For example, when you apply heat to a raw egg, it gets hard, and when you beat cream, you get whipped cream and then butter. Change also relates to the children's sense of their own development and to the different skills they are capable of mastering at different ages.

Interrelationship   For example, animals and people affect each other's survival. They are also affected by the weather. The children may have pets at home and thus experience this concept daily. This concept also relates to the children's dependent role in their families and can be the focus of many discussions.

Adaptation For example, people have adapted to life in different climates. The fur on some animals changes thickness with the seasons. This concept also relates to the children's experiences with the different seasons.

Variation For example, all animals eat to survive, but they eat a variety of different foods. All the children in the class may be about the same age, but they have different tastes, they look different, and they have different abilities.

Energy For example, the food we eat is turned into energy, and moving air can be used to turn a pinwheel. Young children experience different levels of their own energy, and most need a rest after lunch.

Scientific Attitudes

The content of the science curriculum is vast. The emphasis is on developing certain attitudes, not on teaching a body of facts. To encourage these attitudes, the teacher and the children have to:

Have questioning minds
Delight in the process of discovery
Have patience and discipline and be able to see a project through to its conclusion
Observe all aspects of a thing before coming to conclusions
Understand that conclusions are not absolute or everlasting
Realize that much of what we know today was unknown a short while ago and may no longer be true tomorrow
Have open minds and be willing to change their ideas if they are proved incorrect
Know that there is nothing disgraceful about making mistakes—that new questions and discoveries come from mistakes
Be fascinated with the adventure of scientific investigation, without losing sight of the needs of living things and the environment

The Scientific Method

Throughout all scientific investigations in the classroom, the teacher and the children use a general approach that is very much like the scientist's method. This consists of:

Making careful observations
Studying the relationships between things—sorting, grouping, and classifying information

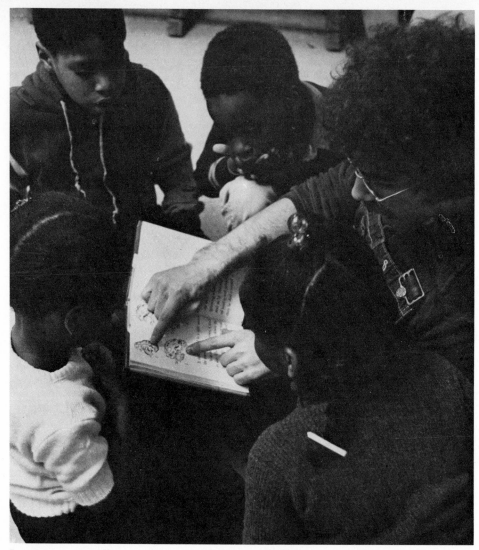

In science, as in all curriculum areas, books are an important resource material.

Formulating precise questions
Experimenting with possible solutions
Keeping accurate records
Creating new concepts that unify the new information
Testing conclusions

The scientific method is closely related to children's natural inclination to wonder, watch, and search for the reason "why." Children find the world a fascinating and mysterious place, and they are eager to make sense out of it. Play is a child's method of learning, and it is often like a scientific study. Like scientists, children at play are constantly using their senses to investigate the likenesses and differences in the things around them. If they are given the freedom to explore, they will seek explanations for things that are confusing or unknown.

The Teacher's Role

While the child's life is rich in possibilities for scientific learning, the teacher plays a crucial role in turning these possibilities into understandings and knowledge. For the classroom to become a laboratory for investigation and discovery, the teacher has to:

Appreciate the children's curiosity and natural inclination to explore the environment and learn about the world.

Believe that play is essential—and act on that belief.

Set the stage. Provide the necessary materials that will stimulate the children to make discoveries.

Be familiar with the materials and some of their possibilities.

Listen to and observe the children carefully to know what questions are important to them.

Use language that will help the children focus on what they are doing and deepen their understanding of the experience. Ask questions when this will stimulate the children's thinking.

Create an atmosphere in which the children feel safe to explore and make mistakes.

While emphasizing firsthand experiences, provide resource people and other sources of information when relevant.

Provide opportunities for the children to repeat experiences and to see the same learning in different settings.

Seek the most accurate information available and be able to put it in terms that the children will understand.

Use a scientific method.

Enjoy the scientific method.

Be able to say, "I don't know, but maybe we can find out."

In general, the teacher needs to "help [the child] learn to go on learning all the rest of his life in a world that does not stand still."* The teacher cannot give the children the specific information they will require in the future, but she can help provide them with the tools they will need to deal with whatever they face. Science in the early childhood

---

*Ruth Roche (coordinator), *Young Children and Science*, Association for Childhood Education International, Washington, 1964, p. 3.

program touches many sensitive and complicated subjects, such as life, sex, aging, and death. The teacher cannot be expected to have all the answers on these subjects for herself or for the children, who are constantly asking probing questions. Yet the teacher does have the responsibility to deal with children honestly and with respect. She needs to understand and overcome her own hesitations about these topics, and when children ask questions, she must be willing to help them find explanations they can accept. In this way, science can truly be part of building children's self-confidence and positive self-image.

SOCIAL STUDIES

Very often the social studies curriculum grows out of spontaneous discussions and activities. For one group of children it started when they came back from a walk outside in the winter air. Many of them were talking about how cold their hands were and how good it felt to come inside to the warm classroom. Yet when the teacher asked them how the room got warm, no one knew. He asked more questions. All the children knew that the radiator was the warmest spot in the room. But no one could make the connection between this fact and the heating system in the building. It was simply outside the children's experience.

The teacher sensed the children's interest and used this as the beginning of a much deeper investigation. He provided the direct experiences that helped the children gain more knowledge of this aspect of the world around them. He took them to the basement, where they saw the furnace. They talked with the janitor and learned that the furnace used oil. They planned to watch a fuel delivery. They located the pipes in the hallway and in the room, and this led them back to the radiator. They also talked about other ways of heating buildings. Every answer seemed to lead them to new questions.

In this way the teacher turned an everyday experience into a much broader study of how people meet their essential needs. This kind of investigation is an example of what social studies for young children can be.

What Is Social Studies?

Children are constantly learning about themselves and their environment. Through a well-planned social studies curriculum, the teacher can help the children organize their experiences and make sense out of them. She can help them expand their ideas and feel more confident and comfortable in what often seems a vast and confusing world.

In the largest sense, social studies is the story of people and their relationships to one another and to their environment—in the past, present, and future. It includes history, geography, economics, politics, and culture. It deals with concepts such as the following:

Who are we? What are our needs? How are we alike? How are we different?

How do we organize our lives? How do we meet our needs? How do we work with others to survive—to get food and shelter, to find security and love, and to deal with our fears? What kinds of groups are we part of? Why? How do we communicate with one another? How do we get from one place to another? What routines, rules, and laws are part of our lives? What kinds of cultures, rituals, and holidays do we have?

How do we influence our environment? What do we create? What do we build? What are our tools? How do we use natural resources to meet our basic needs?

What impact does the environment have on us? What things in nature affect our lives, such as rivers, oceans, and the weather? What man-made things affect us, such as subways and machines?

Social Studies for the Young Child

For the young child, the answers to these abstract questions lie in very real and personal experiences. Every concept needs to be translated into activities that are relevant to the child's world; they need to be related to the child's most familiar surroundings. One teacher found this out when she brought in a map of the world and tried to talk to a group of city children about other countries. She quickly saw that the word *country* meant only trees and grass to most of the children. Although she was very interested in geography, she realized that in order to introduce the subject properly, she would have to work on a map of the classroom with the children and then possibly expand the study to a map of the school and then the block.

As a child grows, his world begins to include more people, places, and things. At first the child's world revolves around himself, his family, and his home. As he increases his understanding of each of these areas, his interests extend further away from himself and his familiar sur-roundings. School enters the picture, and the community becomes more important.

As is true of abstract concepts in all areas of interest to young children, abstract social studies concepts take very concrete forms. For instance, for the young child, the abstract concept "Who are we?" becomes specifically:

Who am I?
What can I feel?
What can I do?
What do I look like?

What do I need to grow?

For the child in his home, this concept becomes:

> With whom do I live?
> Who cares for me?
> What are they like?
> What do they do?
> How are they the same as me and different from me?

For the child in school, it becomes:

> Who takes me to school?
> Who are the people in my class?
> What other people are at my school?
> What do we do there?
> How are these people the same as those at home and different from them?

For the child in the community, it becomes:

> What other people do I see in my neighborhood?
> What do they do?

How Does the Teacher Plan the Social Studies Program?

The possibilities are vast. The focus of the social studies program will vary enormously depending on the specific group of children, the community, and the time in which they live. "How do I get to school?" is answered differently by different children. "How do I get the food I need?" also is answered differently by a child living in a rural town in the Midwest and by a child who lives in a big city. Their tastes may be different, and their experiences are different. It is also true that food is produced, packaged, and marketed very differently today from the way it was only a few years ago, and there is greater interest in nutrition. To plan a program that is both interesting and relevant to the children in the group, the teacher needs to be aware of what they already know. He needs to answer these very basic questions about the children and the community:

> What are the children like? How old are they? What are their concerns? What are their daily experiences? What are their loves, fears, misunderstandings, and doubts?
> What is the community like? What does it look like? Who lives there? What ethnic groups are part of the community? What kinds of work go on

in the community? What services are available to the people? What sources of entertainment does the neighborhood provide? What goes on in the streets? What are the people talking about? What in the community might be of special interest to the children?

For some of the answers to these questions, the teacher needs to:

Listen to the children
Observe them at play
Talk to them
Talk to their parents
Take a walk around the block
Explore the community
Familiarize himself with the many cultures and traditions in the community

Once the teacher has established an area of interest, he needs to:

Find out what the children already know about this topic.
Determine what he already knows about the topic. What experiences has he had that relate to this area of study? How does he feel about exploring it with the children?
Think of all the possible directions the study can take. For example, familiar food, such as milk, can become the center of many explorations (Figure 6-17). Many topics can be subdivided even further.
Decide which areas are the most suitable for, and interesting to, the children in the group.
Do research to find out as much as he can about the topic. This

Figure 6-17
Exploring a familiar topic.

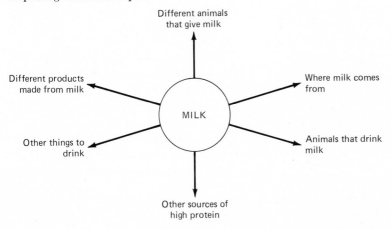

includes gathering information on the adult level as well as resources for the children.

Determine the basic concepts that he wants the children to learn and the best way to have this group of children experience the learning.

Plan direct experiences for the children. What things can he bring into the classroom? What field trips are possible?

Provide related activities that will reinforce or broaden the children's experience.

Social Studies and Dramatic Play

Dramatic play is an essential part of any social studies program. Children learn about themselves and the world around them by trying out the roles and the situations they observe. Play in the housekeeping area can help children clarify and expand their ideas about how they see people live and how they see people relate to one another. The housekeeping area can become an integral part of many social studies investigations; dramatic play is the child's method of research. (See Learning Through Dramatic Play, page 85.)

Social Studies and Blocks

Play in the block area can also be the beginning of many investigations into the home, school, and community. A group of children playing with rubber animals and blocks will often put the lions, cows, and dogs all together. Depending on the children's age and the available resources, the teacher can provide firsthand experiences so that they can learn to sort different animals that are found in different settings. In the same way, small play cars in the block area can lead to a very detailed exploration of streets, garages, neighboring roads, highways, bridges, and tunnels. The variety of play in this area, like the play in the housekeeping area, often depends on the richness of the materials provided. Once the children have begun an investigation of a specific topic, the teacher can add other materials that will stimulate new ideas. For instance, when the children in one group started using blocks and wooden figures to make houses, the teacher added small boxes and other things that they could use for pieces of furniture and accessories.

The block corner can also serve as a place to reinforce ideas. One class that went on a trip to an airport used the blocks to duplicate many of the things they saw. After a return trip to the airport, the construction became even more complex. The children also used the large hollow blocks to make an airplane they could get into, and they acted out an actual flight and a landing at the airport.

This child is recreating with blocks a trip his class took.

Social Studies and the Other Curriculum Areas

Social studies can help give the program a sense of continuity. It can also be a unifying element in the curriculum. The investigation of a single topic may suggest stories to read and write, musical activities, scientific experiments, art activities, and trips. For one group of children who lived near a beach, this important part of their environment became the focus of a study that lasted throughout the year and brought in all the curriculum areas.

The topic of study began one day early in the year when a group of children playing in the housekeeping area decided to take a trip to the beach. They packed a basket of (plastic) food, walked out of the housekeeping area, sat down in the middle of the room, and had a great time pretending to swim and picnic. They repeated this activity several times, and most of the other children got involved. *With the teacher's guidance this spontaneous activity developed into:*

Making a book about foods you can take on a picnic, using pictures cut out of magazines

Taking trips to the beach, which included collecting shells and other things found there; digging in the sand and looking at the sand at various levels; shifting the sand; looking at the beach at different seasons; taking photographs at the beach of people, birds, etc; and making a tape recording of sounds heard at the beach

Making up a story, using the photographs from the trips

Sorting the shells

Matching the shells to pictures in a book about shells

Reading stories about the beach

Creating songs, using familiar tunes but with new words about the trips to the beach

Using the small shells in mathematical games

Playing lotto by matching shells and silhouettes of shells

Filling a small tub with sand and exploring it both wet and dry

Using found objects like shells and seaweed to make collages

Using different-colored sand for designs

Reenacting the trips to the beach

Setting up both a saltwater and a freshwater aquarium, which was the beginning of a whole new investigation of fish and of animals who live in or near water and of the food we get from different bodies of water

This kind of social studies investigation is a statement to children about the interrelationship of all areas of knowledge. It demonstrates to children that learning is a process and that their curiosity can continually lead them to exciting new discoveries. It encourages children to express themselves, to ask questions, and to constantly explore their environment. In this way, social studies can help children feel comfortable with themselves and the world around them.

MUSIC

In a classroom where the children are deeply involved in their play, you will often hear a song, a chant, or a hummed melody. It may be a television commercial being sung in the housekeeping area or a repeated phrase which one child made up and which is then chanted by the group. But music will be a part of every day in a busy, creative atmosphere.

For young children, music is not necessarily a formal melody or game. It is many different kinds of experiences with sound and rhythm. Music is sound created by using the body or something found in the environment. It is also a bodily response to sound. Music is in all of us, and it is an important part of every culture. The early childhood curriculum builds on the many different aspects of music. It includes listening, singing, and movement experiences. It uses folk, classical, and popular music, and it includes games played by many different groups of people here and around the world.

Musical Development

Even before the child talks, he finds pleasure in making a variety of sounds with his mouth. The infant loves to bang two things together, to hit the bars of his crib, to clap his hands, and to imitate sounds. He may bounce up and down to the radio, and he loves to listen to a lullaby or to be rocked and swayed in a grown-up's arms. All this is part of the child's musical development.

The child needs to be able to explore movement and sound without any adult pressure for achievement or conformity. The child's creativity and enjoyment will be stifled if he is pressured to clap exactly on beat, to sing the words and music accurately, or to move the way the teacher says to move, rather than the way he feels like moving.

Goals of the Music Program

As in all creative activities, teachers do not seek to develop professional singers or dancers. Instead, music and movement are presented as ways of expressing many emotions and thoughts. The focus is not on the product but on the experience itself—the process and how the process supports learning and growth. The purpose of the music program is to encourage the children's development in all areas.

Physical goals

To allow them to discover a means of expression that uses the entire body

To help them develop greater control over their actions and creations

Emotional goals

To help them gain self-confidence by allowing them to develop their own ideas

To encourage them to get pleasure from the music they learn and create

Intellectual goals

To link creative expression to other aspects of cognitive growth

To help them be inventive

To encourage them to find a variety of ways of combining and organizing the music they make

To encourage a sensitivity to the sounds around them

Social goals

To help them find positive ways of interacting with one another

To help them become part of a group

To create a group sense through enjoyable, shared experiences

To allow for the acceptance of individuality within the group

The Teacher's Role

In order to develop the children's musical abilities it is most important for the teacher to create an atmosphere in which each child is encouraged to make his or her own unique contribution. Even the shyest or most anxious children will feel freer to participate when they feel comfortable doing things in their own way and when their contributions are not judged as right or wrong. The emphasis is not on everyone doing something the same way, but on the variety of individual efforts. When the children are moving to music, the teacher can point out how "Karen is moving her hands from side to side" or how "Joe is using his shoulders in a different way."

In general, the teacher:

Appreciates the children's natural abilities and interest in music

Uses the children's spontaneous expressions as a springboard for other activities

Tries to stimulate the children's inventiveness

Makes suggestions that help the children make further discoveries

Introduces songs, music or musical instruments any time during the day when this can add to what the children are already doing

Plans musical activities that help the children become aware of all the elements of music

Uses music every day as part of the planned activities
Does not judge the children's efforts
Does not force children to participate until they are ready

The Different Elements of the Music Program

The music curriculum should help the children to develop an awareness of sound and of how it can be combined in different rhythms, melodies, and forms. This curriculum includes both making and responding to music in several ways.

Listening Developing listening skills is as basic to musical development as it is to children's overall cognitive development. *Auditory discrimination*—the ability to tell the differences between sounds—is part of determining and responding to music that is fast or slow, high or low, loud or soft, or happy or sad. It is also the foundation of phonics. As in other areas of cognitive development, the larger discriminations come first, and the finer ones appear later. Young children enjoy trying to identify the different sounds of familiar animals; they also like to guess sounds in the environment that they hear on records or on a tape they have recorded outside. They can try to guess the names of other children from the sound of their voices, or they can try to identify the sound of a familiar musical instrument hidden behind a screen. In using musical instruments, listening skills are required only to play particular phrases or to find the beat of a song.

If a record player and records are available, the children will enjoy choosing music to listen to while they are playing in other parts of the room. The teacher can also use different records during playtime and rest time, and she can help the children become accustomed to the different moods that music can evoke.

Singing In selecting songs, the appeal and meaning to the children are of the utmost importance. Songs should relate to the interests of the group. Those with repeated phrases are easier for young children to learn. It is not necessary to have a vast list of songs. It is better to have a few songs that can be adapted to the children's needs. Whenever possible, the children should be encouraged to make up words to familiar songs. "Jingle Bells" could be "Donna Builds," for example:

Donna builds,
Donna builds,
Donna builds a store.
And then she takes another block
To give the store a door.

Teachers and children share a dramatic moment through music.

Children especially like songs that use their names. With a little creativity, the teacher can find ways to use the children's names in the songs they know. "Where Is Thumbkin?" can be used with the children's first names ("Where Is David?"), and "Michael, Row the Boat Ashore" is a good song for telling about the things the children did at playtime ("Sally Painted a Picture Today").

Songs also help promote language development. Some songs involve pointing to parts of the body; others imitate the sounds of animals and things. The rhyming in songs is a vital part of reading skills. After a song is learned, children enjoy putting their own words to the melody. Cumulative songs develop memory and sequence skills. In these songs younger children can follow pictures drawn from left to right to reinforce directionality (or left-to-right orientation). With songs using dialogue, the children can be broken up into different groups, or the teacher and the children can take different parts.

Songs also provide or reinforce information if the teacher helps the children understand all the words.

When introducing a new song, the teacher doesn't have the children learn it line by line, nor does she stress the melody or pronunciation of each word. By repeating it over and over for a period of time in different appropriate settings, the children will pick it up and make it their own.

Using musical instruments As the children spontaneously tap on tables, rub a piece of wood with sandpaper, or stamp their feet as they walk outside, the teacher can point out the sounds and rhythms they make. This helps the children feel that they can make music with their bodies and with things found in the environment.

There should also be some basic musical instruments available to the children. Drums, tambourines, and bells can be set out on a table or hung on a pegboard within the children's reach so that they can use them spontaneously in their play. The children should be encouraged to find a variety of ways of using instruments. They should feel that, within certain guidelines, any experimentation is possible. From time to time new instruments can be introduced. Xylophones, maracas, cymbals, triangles, and bells are other instruments that children enjoy. They also like to explore the different variations of one instrument. There are many different kinds of drums from different cultures. They are played in many ways and make a wide range of sounds.

The children can become comfortable using the names of the familiar instruments. Various games can be played for this purpose, or the teacher can use a familiar song; "Did You Ever See a Lassie?" becomes "Did You Ever Hear a Drum?" and "Old MacDonald Had a Farm" becomes "Old MacDonald Had a Band."

There are many different objects that the children can bring from home and use as music makers. Empty boxes, pans, and a grater all can be used to make a variety of sounds. The children can also make their own musical instruments. Rhythm sticks, sand blocks, coffee-can drums, rubber-band guitars, and paper-cup maracas are all examples of musical instruments that young children can make from a few simple, on-hand materials.

When introducing instruments at group time, the teacher can pass them from child to child, encouraging each child to discover what sounds can be made. For a group music time, certain ground rules need to be established. There should be some agreed-upon signal for starting and stopping. Using musical instruments with a familiar song sets up a natural beginning and end. Children enjoy using instruments to accompany songs. In a song like "The Eensy Weensy Spider," each line can be played by a different group of children with a certain instrument. This helps give some order to the use of musical instruments in a group. The children can sing "one, two, three, four" to "Jingle Bells" and play drums on the first beat, bells on the third beat, or any other such variation.

Musical instruments can also be used to accompany stories. For instance, in the story "Goldilocks and the Three Bears," each character in the story is represented by a musical instrument, and that instrument is played every time that character is mentioned.

There is no one special time to use instruments. The children should feel that they can use them as part of many other activities, like dramatic play in the housekeeping area or the block area.

Movement   In all aspects of movement the children's individual contributions should be recognized and respected. The children should be encouraged to be as inventive in the use of their bodies as they are in all other aspects of music. While sitting on the floor, the teacher can ask each child in the circle to find a different way to move a part of his or her body. Even when the children are simply walking to music, the teacher can point out how a child is moving his or her hands and can ask the other children to try this and then find a way of their own.

The mood and rhythm of music elicit different responses in different people. The children must be allowed this freedom to react with their entire bodies to what they hear and feel. If the teacher says, "March now; run now," the children will respond to her verbal directions, not to the music. This procedure removes the possibility for perceptual learning and does not allow for an emotional response to the music. Walking, running, galloping, crawling, rolling, hopping, and (for older children) skipping are all basic movements that children enjoy. The way they walk, run, gallop, etc., will vary, depending on their individual responses to the music, which may be fast, slow, heavy, light, sad, or gay. The children should also have experiences discovering their own way of moving to a variety of different kinds of music from different cultures.

Sometimes a prop like a ball, hoop, rope, balloon, scarf, or piece of crepe paper can stimulate individual creative movement to music. These props help some children feel more comfortable with this kind of unstructured activity. There are times when a little structure can help release a great deal of energy and creativity. If the teacher or a child alternates calling "Move" or "Freeze," the children may find it easier to try out some different ways of letting go.

Language can also be the inspiration for movement improvisation. The children can find their own way to act out different animals or things in the environment, such as an airplane, a spaceship, a typewriter, or a snowstorm. They can try using their whole bodies to express different words like *happy*, *sad*, *light*, *heavy*, *yes*, and *no*. They can pretend to be walking through things like water, snow, tall grass, or mud or to be making their way across a frozen pond.

Many group games also provide enjoyable movement experiences. Some, like Ha-Ha This A-Way, allow for some degree of individuality, as each child has a turn making his or her own motion. In this kind of game the teacher should be especially sensitive to the shy or withdrawn child who finds it difficult to perform in full view of the group. It should be understood that some children may refuse to take a turn at all but if they do have the courage to enter the circle, the slightest motion should be recognized as the child's contribution to the game.

Using Music in the Classroom

The different aspects of the music program can be used throughout the day. They can also be part of a special group time. This might include some singing, possibly the addition of some instruments, and then a group movement experience using basic rhythms, a game, or an improvisation. The length of this group time and the variety of experience will depend on the children's age, the number of children, the level of their energy, and their interests. Whatever the selection of activities or the time at which music is used, the emphasis should be on the development of the children's creativity.

Other Benefits of Music

Music is useful in the development of other aspects of the program.

Music enriches other curriculum areas   Music can link different elements of the curriculum. Songs can relate to a recent social studies topic, and they can help promote language development and reinforce mathematical concepts. Ideas that come up in dramatic play can be further expanded in song, music, and movement.

Music helps individual children   Music can help in the initial separation between parent and child. The child can be encouraged to become part of the group by joining in a familiar song. Music can also help individual children establish a relationship to the group. It can help an active child organize his or her energies. It can help a shy child make a contribution to the group.

Music helps establish and maintain routines   Music can sometimes be used to signal the approach of clean-up and can encourage the children to put their work away. The children can also sing or use simple chants as transitions from one activity to another. There can be songs that the children sing as they walk from one place to another or a special song to greet everyone in the morning and say good-bye at the end of the day.

Music helps develop the children's positive self-image   Improvised songs that use the children's names, refer to parts of their bodies, or describe their clothing or activities can give them a good feeling about themselves. Music can also give each child an opportunity to make a contribution to the group. The children can also follow one another's rhythm or motion. Using songs from different cultures also supports the children's feeling of self-worth.

Music helps form a bridge between home and school   Music can create a bond between home and school. The parents can be asked to share their favorite songs or bring in their musical instruments. The children can be encouraged to sing melodies that they have learned at home. This can help them appreciate their own culture. It can also help them see the variety of ways in which people can express themselves.

ART

Children's Art: The Creative Process

"Art is valuable because it is a means of self-expression. It is a language to express feelings—to draw off tensions or to express well-being. The young child needs avenues of expression. His speech is limited. His feelings are strong."*

If we agree that there is a need for "avenues of expression," then we must be concerned with establishing a climate that puts our practice where our theory is. To do this, we must understand the creative process, for if we understand it, we will not interfere with it.

A child uses materials in different ways during the following three stages of the development of the creative process:

Exploration (the manipulative or kinesthetic stage)   In this stage the child explores a medium and learns its capabilities. He scribbles, he bangs and breaks clay, and he makes drips and lines with paint.

Intuitive design (transitional stage)   During this phase the child exploring an art medium will see a shape or form in the material that suggests something to him. A curved line may suggest a face, or a thin role of clay may suggest a snake.

Intended design (realistic or representational stage)   At this point the child decided in advance what he wants to make and then draws, paints, or models his subject.

A child may remain at any one stage for a certain length of time or may move back and forth between these stages. One child may work for awhile at the third stage, for example, and then revert to the first. The stage at which a child works at any one time will reflect his or her needs, although age and experience with art media will also be influencing factors. All children should have an opportunity to experiment.

---

*Katherine Read, *The Nursery School: A Human Relationships Laboratory*, 5th ed., Saunders, Philadelphia, 1971, p. 76.

Creating her own puppet gives a child an opportunity for personal expression.

Let us examine these stages closely and see how we can support children during them.

Exploration

"Here is a ball of clay," you say. Let the child handle the clay. If the child does nothing, you may say, "Let me show you what it is." You can squeeze it, bang it, break it apart, and put it together again before suggesting, "Here, you try it."

What would you do if you had never handled clay before? You might push your finger in it and make a hole; you might break off little pieces; or you might roll the clay in your hands or on the table and give it a squeeze. It's really lots of fun! Suppose, though, that while you are doing one of these things, someone comes along and says, warmly and with interest, "What are you making?" The question might spoil it all for you. You were just having fun, and then this person made you feel silly because you were not making anything. You might even stop exploring the medium.

Suppose no one comes along, and you continue to play with the clay and enjoy it. Suddenly the material seems to suggest a form that interests you, one that you can identify. "Look," you might shout, "a dog!"

Intended Design

Then one day when you are working with clay, you take the next step. "I'm going to make a dog," you say, and you begin with this intention. Just as you are finishing the dog, however, someone comes along and says, "That squirrel is great!" Or someone might ask, "What is it?" when you thought it was clearly a dog. The questions "What is it?" and "What are you making?" are destructive to the creative process.

Supporting Creativity

It is vitally important to a child's physical, intellectual, social, and emotional development that a teacher never interfere with his or her free use of art media. Let us suppose that instead of allowing you to play around with a ball of clay, I showed it to you and said, "Look, this is clay. I can make a basket with it." Then suppose that after I made one, I handed the clay to you and said, "You make something." If what I did looked too hard to you or if the basket looked too good, you might refuse to touch the clay. On the other hand, if it seemed like something you could do, you might take the clay and try to make another basket. This might also happen if I sat at the table where you were handling the clay and made a basket with my clay.

Have you not met adults who can only make baskets with clay because a basket became an achievable goal that had been set long ago? Such an approach eliminates the stage of exploration and manipulation with the medium and interferes with the creative use of material. Adults who are only basket makers can break away from this restraint. Given the opportunity to take a ball of clay and squeeze and bang it, they will quickly experience the explorative and intuitive design stages and begin to enjoy creative work.

The creative process takes place in work with all art media. If you give a child paint for the first time, he will just experiment with it on paper. He may cover the whole sheet first, or he may make dots or lines; then he may see a shape.

Art media are many things to young children. If we look at the scribbling done by children, we notice how very different the scribbles of each child are. Some use a firm, strong line; some make sharp, short lines; and some draw delicate pencil lines. Some children use the entire sheet of paper; others use only one corner. In all these variations, the individuality of each child is evident, and each child has a great need to use the medium to express himself, to communicate, to release some feelings.

Each child draws only what is significant to him. A child is not involved in drawing what he sees. He sees that a house is bigger than a person, but he may draw the person much bigger than the house because that is what is meaningful to him. When he draws a picture of a family, the size of each member of the family reflects not what he sees but what he feels. He may make the infant the biggest, or Mommy may tower over everyone (Figure 6-18). Throughout history, in all cultures and in all societies, we find that children's first representational drawings reveal what they consider to be the most significant parts of their bodies, such as the face, arms, or legs. The trunk appears in children's drawings much later, and the unimportant neck has to wait even longer. As Joseph DiLeo noted:

> The issue of timelessness has led to comparisons with the art of prehistoric man. The irrelevance of place is claimed by those who have noted identical characteristics in drawings by children from far away places. Drawings by children from diverse racial groups are strikingly familiar, as are those by children from a variety of social environments.*

Educators should be concerned with the creative process, for the finished product fades in importance and is frequently deceptive. Consider this example: Five-year-old Johnny was painting at an easel, reliving his experience of seeing a store hold-up. He chatted to himself the entire time, and the teacher was fortunate enough to hear him. Johnny had painted many figures on the paper, and as he painted, he said, "The robbers came and took out their guns; the cops came and took out their guns." The painting, at this point, was quite realistic and amazing. "Then the bullets got shot and went all over." Excited, Johnny was now sweeping his brush back and forth across the paper. His finished product was a big blob of paint that was turning very brown and beginning to tear through the paper; all the figures and guns were hidden under a thick layer of "bullets and blood."

The process of expressing this terrifying experience was extremely important for Johnny, extending into his need to express his feelings about the bullets and the blood. The finished product? It was a mess. Yet who would have dared to interfere with this child's needs? Who could have pulled that painting away before the blood was spilled in order to rescue a "beautiful product"?

Another example is four-year-old Kim, who always painted two fine

---

*Joseph H. DiLeo, *Children's Drawings as Diagnostic Aids*, Brunner/Mazel, New York, 1973.

Mommy   Daddy.   Me   brother

Figure 6-18

A drawing by Debbie, a four-year-old, of her family. Her teacher's comment reads: "Debbie's mother is a rather small, thin woman. She appears so large here because that is Debbie's perception of her mother in the family."

figures. She would then smear and blot out one of them. The product was always rather messy by our adult standards. But Kim was a twin. The art experience gave her the opportunity to act out her feelings. I think we can all see that this was a good way for her to do it. Figure 6-19 shows drawings by a pair of five-year-old twins.

If a child is permitted to explore freely the use and possibilities of art

Figure 6-19

A pair of drawings by five-year-old twin girls. Of her drawing (*top*), one twin said: "A monster is coming to get the girl." Then, her teacher reports, "Right next to the monster, she started another figure, but she eliminated it." The other twin said: "I made two girls" (*bottom*).

media, he or she will be able to have satisfactory experiences with them. If you interfere with any part of this natural process, you may distort it and delay the time when the child will really enjoy a creative experience with these materials. Because they give a child a picture to fill in, patterns, tracings, and coloring books also interfere with the natural process.

When you admire the work that a child has done, be sure that you are admiring something real. If you try to fool a child, he or she will know it; valid comments might be, "That color is so red," "That line has a nice curve," or "That line is so straight." An unloaded question you might ask is, "Would you like to tell me about it?" (See Figure 6-20.) This gives the child the right to say "no."

Figure 6-20

This drawing—by Vera, a five-year-old—looks like a happy, sunny garden. But when she was asked by her teacher, "Would you like to tell me about it?" Vera said, "The flower ate the girl up and the sun made her better. Then it ate her up again, and the sun couldn't help anymore."

Remember, we don't expect all children to become artists or sculptors, but we should try to give them enjoyable, satisfactory creative experiences. Children can do wonderful things, and they will weave wonderful stories around what they have done. And we should, of course, be delighted to write these stories down as they are told and then read them back to the children.

Carl Rogers's description of the creative process is excellent:

> My definition, then, of the creative process is that it is the emergence in action of a novel relational product growing out of the uniqueness of the individual on the one hand, the materials, events, people, or circumstances of his life on the other.*

As children grow older, sensitive and skilled teachers will be able to teach techniques to those who have really learned to enjoy art media. Adults who are afraid to draw or paint are people who have never had an opportunity to discover how much fun there is in working freely with materials. They were never allowed to experience the creative process. They have been robbed of a great outlet and experience that could have served them throughout their lives. Let's not allow this to happen to children.

DO'S	DON'TS
Understand that when children draw huge hands, construct unreal proportions, or leave out items that you might consider essential, they are concentrating on what is important to them at the moment. Their work should be accepted as they create it. Often observing what is emphasized or omitted will give you an important insight into a child's development.	Don't correct or add to a child's work.
Help the children to feel confident about their work and to take pride in it. Stress the individuality of each creation.	Don't compare the children's work or show preferences. Don't allow their comment on other children's work—"Oh,

---

*Carl Rogers, "Towards a Theory of Creativity," in Harold Anderson (ed.), *Creativity and Its Cultivation*, Harper & Row, New York, 1959.

DO'S	DON'TS
Respect the many different ideas children have, as they use the same materials.	that's just scribble scrabble"—to go unnoticed. You can respond by saying, "That's John's design" or "That's his idea."
Display art work in its original form at the child's eye level so that he can be aware of its presence. Matting the children's paintings shows your interest and pride in their accomplishments. Ask a child whether he wishes his work to be displayed or would like to take it home. A child's work has individual meaning for him and must be treated carefully.	Don't hang or display the children's artwork too high. Don't discard their work without checking with them.
Tell the children why you like their work; comment on the red line near the blue circles or mention the three blue dots. Commenting on what you see helps the children become more consciously aware of their work. Help the children think about what they want to paint, draw, build, or model; for example, ask, "How does a cow eat?" or "How many legs does the animal have?"	Don't ask a child, "What is that?" Don't even try to guess. Don't casually say that a painting or drawing is "beautiful," "great," or "terrific." This does not make a child aware of his or her individuality. Don't make models for the children, even when they protest that they "can't do it." They cannot possibly duplicate what an adult has created. Your model is a way of saying, "I know you are not able to do a good job."
Provide a wide variety of materials so that each child can make a real choice. Remember that selecting their own materials gives the children the opportunity to further develop their self-concepts.	Don't make choices for the children.

DO'S	DON'TS
Offer the children open-ended materials (paint, clay, crayons, wood, blocks) so that they may make discoveries for themselves; this will help them meet their intellectual and emotional needs.	Don't offer coloring books or precut patterns to the children. These are just another way of saying, "You are not capable; you do not have the ability."
Understand that children's co-ordination and muscle development will grow as a result of creating their own artwork. Art for the young child is a developmental process that provides the opportunity for physical, emotional, intellectual, and social growth.	Don't believe that coloring in pictures in a coloring book or cutting on lines that you have drawn will improve a child's coordination.
Remember that the children need continuity. They will not be bored if you offer them opportunities to paint, draw, build, paste, and model every day. Personal growth takes place through repeated experiences with open-ended materials.	Don't offer a particular art material once a week. Children need an ongoing experience with the material so that new growth and discoveries can be made.
Remember that, for the young child, the process involved in the creation is all-important. Parents can be helped to understand this and to appreciate and accept their children's work.	Don't feel that the final product must "look" like something— that it must be distinguishable to an adult's eye, especially to the eye of a parent.

Basic materials are purchased most economically in quantity from a school supply firm. Some of this material is offered daily and should be stored on easily accessible shelves and containers. You should provide the following:

Drawing paper, (12- by 18-inch manila paper is recommended for crayons, chalk, paint, collages, cutting, pasting, etc.).
Large crayons.

Scissors (include a few left-handed pairs).
Several sizes of colored construction paper.
Paste, glue, or both.
Paper punch.
Newsprint paper (18 by 24 inches) for painting.
Masking tape and cellophane tape.
Tissue paper.
Cellophane.
Paintbrushes. Provide brushes from $3/4$ to 1 inch line and from $1/4$ to $1/2$ inch wide so that the children can experiment with lines of different thicknesses.
Tempera paints, dry or prepared. These are cheapest when bought in large quantities. The primary colors should be offered so that the children can mix any color they wish.
Staplers.
Finger paints (see the recipes on page 164).
Clay (moist water clay is best).
Water to paint with outside. Use with cans or buckets and large household-type brushes.
Wallpaper books (for painting, cutting, pasting, etc.).
Lumber and real tools for woodworking (saws, a vise, hammers, nails, free wood from a lumberyard).
Colored chalk (chalk 1 inch in diameter is recommended).
Felt markers.
Pencils.
Large-eyed needles.
Yarn.
Burlap.
Needlepoint mesh.
Fabric.
Fabric scraps (provide many different textures as well as solids and prints), ribbons, rickrack, fur, etc.
Scraps of fancy paper, wrapping paper, etc.
Corregated cardboard and shirt cardboards.
Buttons, beads, and broken necklaces.
Feathers, broomstraws, wire, and place mats.
Wool, string, and cotton thread.
Pipe cleaners, straws, and picture wire.
Lace, paper doilies, and old greeting-card pictures.
Seeds.
Leaves.
Acorns.
Dried flowers.
Bark.
Shells.

Pebbles.

Eggshells.

Nutshells.

Chicken or turkey bones.

Weeds.

Cardboard boxes, all sizes (for sawing and for making boats, houses, trains, a play store, etc.).

Paper bags (for making dolls, puppets, and containers for playing store).

Toilet-paper rolls.

Ice-cream and cottage-cheese containers.

Spools and popsicle sticks.

Cans and jars.

Sawdust (for making collages and modeling—free from a lumberyard).

Soap flakes (for painting and modeling).

Newspapers (to protect floors and tabletops).

Bottle and jar tops (to use as wheels).

Egg cartons.

Paper plates and aluminum plates.

Felt for a feltboard, pictures, collages, etc.

Clothespins (for making dolls and for woodworking).

Sandpaper (to paint on and make chalk drawings on and for woodworking and rubbing designs).

Crepe paper.

Food coloring (for dyes).

Styrofoam (to combine with dowels, twigs, pipe cleaners, etc., for sculpture).

Materials for making print designs (anything dipped in paint and printed on paper)—sponges, felt, gadgets, and leaves.

Paper clips and rubber bands.

Sponges (for making prints and for cleaning).

Large fasteners ($1\frac{1}{2}$ to 2-inch fasteners will hold cardboard boxes together).

Art Recipes and Formulas

Play dough

2 parts flour
1 part salt

Add water. Paint or food coloring may be added to the water. You may also add oil of cloves or 1 tablespoon salad oil.

Sawdust mix

> 4 parts sawdust
> 1 part wheat paste

Add water. Mix well.

Paste

> 1 part flour
> 4 parts water

Cook until clear.

Finger paint (instant)

> $1\frac{1}{2}$ cups liquid starch
> Food coloring
> $1\frac{1}{2}$ cups soap flakes
> 1 quart water

Mix well.

Finger paint (cooked)

> 2 cups sifted flour
> 2 teaspoons salt
> 3 cups cold water

Beat well. Add 2 cups hot water. Cook until thick, divide, and add vegetable dye or tempera.

Fixative (for chalk)

> 1 part shellac
> 2 parts denatured alcohol

Put into a sprayer. This should be made and used only by the teacher.

HEALTH AND PHYSICAL EDUCATION

Helping children reach their fullest potential includes maintaining their good physical health. You will find it helpful and often necessary to become familiar with the current information from the health field. When measles and polio vaccine were finally developed, teachers played an important role in educating parents to the need of immunizing their children. Currently there is grave concern about the harmful effects of food coloring and food additives. There is a growing body of evidence that these substances may be linked to hyperkinesis (hyperactivity in children). The medical profession is now alerting parents to the fact that a person's lifetime eating pattern is established during the early childhood years. Feeding children cake, candy, starch, and highly seasoned foods establishes unhealthy eating habits that may result in poor health. Such habits are hard to break. Eating habits are also culturally determined. It is possible to respect a child's cultural preferences and still maintain nutritional standards. Teachers should serve snacks that reflect their knowledge of nutritional needs. Fruit juices need not be sweetened. Some cookies are more nutritional than others; raisins are sweet and fun to eat; and raw vegetables such as carrots are delicious, healthy snacks. Snack time should be pleasant and relaxed.

Involving parents in cooking events in school can be one way of educating them about nutritional needs. It also gives them an opportunity to share their cultural food preferences with the class.

When the children cook, they learn about the need for cleanliness when handling food and when eating.

If the children spend the entire day in the school, it is necessary to establish routines that allow for adequate rest. Watch for children who become overtired. It is important to be alert to behavior that may indicate illness; a child who seems to be sick should be separated from the other children to help avoid the spread of the illness to the entire group and to help the child feel more comfortable.

Common Concerns about Children's Health and Physical Welfare

Teachers are in the best position to pick up on certain physical problems in the early childhood years. The teacher may not make a diagnosis. She either reports her findings to the school nurse (if the school has one) or notes the symptoms to the parents and suggests that they seek medical attention.

Physical Symptoms That You Should Be Aware Of

Eyes   An eye examination is indicated if a child holds things close to his face, brings his face close to his work, blinks or squints, or trips over things. A child who closes one eye to focus may have an eye condition that can be helped only in the preschool years.

Ears   A child who turns or tilts his head to one side when listening or who always asks "What?" should have an ear examination.

Eating fruit outdoors is healthy and fun.

Urination   A child who urinates often or drinks a lot of water should have a medical examination that includes a urine or blood analysis. The child may have a bladder infection or may be diabetic. Only a doctor can make the diagnosis.

Contagious Skin Ailments

Impetigo   This is a highly contagious skin disease. A child with suspected impetigo needs to be excluded from the class. The disease starts as an itchy blister, which oozes and then forms a yellow crust. It spreads on the child and to other children.

Ringworm   This skin disease is also highly contagious. In the scalp, it spreads out in a ring as it appears to heal in the center. It causes hair to break off. It may appear in the scalp or on the face or other skin areas. On the skin it appears as a round scaly patch.

Conjunctivitis (pinkeye)   This is a highly contagious disease. The eye glues shut with pus. The white of the eye is inflamed, and the inner part of the lower lid is very red. (Allergic reactions which are not contagious cause similar symptoms.)

Lice   Lice attach themselves to the hair. The eggs (nits) look like dandruff. Unlike dandruff, however, the eggs attach themselves to the hair and cannot be blown away. The child scratches his head. Lice are highly contagious.

Allergies

Conditions such as hives, asthma, rhinitis (running nose not caused by a cold), eczema and other skin reactions, and some forms of stomach distress when allergic in base are not contagious. They are caused by an individualized sensitivity to a normally harmless substance. The histamine balance is upset. The doctor often treats allergies with antihistamines.

The most common allergens (a substance to which a person can be allergic) are:

1   Food, such as eggs, chocolate, fish, nuts, wheat, and strawberries
2   Substances that we breathe, such as dust, pollen, and feathers
3   Things that we touch, such as poison ivy, animal hair, and some soaps and deodorants

A person can be allergic to anything. The list above includes only the most common allergens.

Children usually know what they are allergic to and try to avoid the offending substance. The teacher must help in this.

First Aid

Teachers are not allowed to treat children. You may not remove a splinter or try to take anything from a child's eye or nose. To do so may cause harm. A doctor must be consulted.

Cuts   Cuts can be washed with water, and then a Band-Aid or similar bandage may be applied. You may not use any medication on cuts. Soap should not be used.

Bleeding   To stop bleeding, press the cut with a sterile pad. If possible, it is helpful to elevate the affected part if bleeding is very heavy.

Nosebleeds   Keep the child seated. Press the nostril gently after telling the child to breathe through his mouth. If this doesn't stop the bleeding, try ice against the back of the neck or cold, wet cloths over the child's nose. Prolonged or frequent nosebleeds require medical attention.

Epilepsy

There are apt to be children in your class who experience grand mal or petit mal seizures.

Grand mal   In this form of epilepsy the child has a severe seizure. Be calm. Calm your group and assure them that the child is sick and will get better. Place the child on the floor or on a rug or a bed. Remove anything nearby that the child could hit himself against, such as furniture or other objects. If something soft is available, place it under the head. Tilt the chin up and the head to one side. *Do not* insert anything in the child's mouth. *Do not* restrain the body convulsions. Remember that this child has an illness. *Do not* treat the epileptic child differently from the way you treat the other children in the course of the normal, day-to-day activities.

Petit mal   This form of epilepsy is often discovered by teachers of early childhood classrooms. There is no real visible change in the child. There is no convulsion. The child appears to be daydreaming or staring. The episode lasts a few seconds. A child may have many such episodes in the course of the day. He does not know he has been detached from what is going on, which results in his hearing the beginning and end of statements with no knowledge that he has missed the middle. This condition seriously interferes with learning and often remains unnoticed for years.

Common Communicable Diseases

Communicable childhood diseases usually have an incubation period lasting from ten days to three weeks after exposure. This varies with each illness. Children are not contagious during this incubation period and usually cannot be excluded from the classroom. The following table lists and describes the most common early childhood diseases.

Disease	First Signs	Incubation Period	Prevention	How Long Contagious	Degree of Seriousness
Chicken pox	Mild fever, 36 hours later, small raised pimples, filled with fluid, ap-	From 2 to 3 weeks; usually 13 to 17 days.	None. Immunity follows illness.	From 1 day before appearance to 6 days after appearance of last rash.	Not serious. Very uncomfortable.

Disease	First Signs	Incubation Period	Prevention	How Long Contagious	Degree of Seriousness
	pear. There are usually three waves of pox pimples on different days.				
German measles	Mild or no fever. Sometimes accompanied by mild cold or enlarged glands at the back of the neck.	From 2 to 3 weeks; usually 16 to 18 days.	Vaccine.	From 7 days before appearance of rash until rash fades, approximately five days later.	Generally not serious except in pregnant women.
Measles	Rising temperature. Dry cough. Nose runs and eyes become red 3 to 4 days before appearance of rash.	From 1 to 2 weeks; usually 10 to 12 days.	Vaccine (a must).	From 5 to 9 days—4 days before rash appears and 5 days after rash goes. Contagious at first sign of cold.	Treacherous; can result in death or cause brain damage.
Mumps	Fever, headache, and vomiting. Painful swollen glands. May start on one side.	From 11 to 26 days; usually 18 days.	Vaccine.	From 1 to 2 days before onset until all swelling on both sides is gone.	Serious in males after puberty.

Outdoor Play

Children need active play and quiet play. They need fresh air.

The "great outdoors" is truly the setting for exciting play experiences for children. It offers them the opportunity to refresh themselves physically and to test out newly acquired skills like climbing, skipping, hopping, jumping, balancing, and running. In a large, open, safe space outdoors, children have an excellent chance to practice these physical skills and further develop their concept of themselves as capable people. Gaining control of their bodies—making their arms and legs do what they want them to do—gives children a feeling of mastery and achievement.

Although we recognize the many advantages of the outdoor setting, not every child will feel comfortable in the playground. Observe one child for ten minutes indoors; then observe the same child outdoors. What differences do you see? With some children, the change is slight; with others, the difference is dramatic. The less structured, open space provided outdoors may overwhelm some children. They do not know what to do. They feel uneasy moving about, climbing, running, and jumping. These children will need the teacher's support and encouragement outdoors. When they are able to climb to the top of the jungle gym or jump from the top step of the stairs, they will feel more confident and might venture to try some activity inside that is less structured. Children who are not as active indoors might feel less confined outdoors and exhibit a great deal of spontaneous, active play in their new setting. This kind of information is helpful to teachers. It gives them a deeper insight into the individual child and enables them to plan more effectively for each child's needs. In the case of a child who is less involved indoors than outside, the teacher can build on that child's demonstrated physical skills. He might encourage the child to teach another child to do what she can do. If the teacher discusses with the child what he has seen of her physical abilities, this provides her with feedback that will add to her development of a positive self-image. These positive feelings might encourage the child to try something more challenging indoors, perhaps painting, completing a puzzle, or adding her comments to a group discussion.

It is important to spend some time each day outdoors. Of course, the most pleasant seasons to be outside are summer, spring, and fall, but the winter months offer some exciting and exhilarating times for children, and outdoor play at this time should not be avoided. Parents can be advised that the children in your school go out in all kinds of weather and need to come to school appropriately dressed. For parents who express concern about the health of their children in cold or rainy weather, the U.S. Department of Health, Education and Welfare provides a wealth of information about the value of outdoor play in all kinds of weather. Teachers can also point out the excellent educational opportunities provided by a walk in the rain or a trek in the newly fallen snow.

Children need to play outdoors. They need to move around freely, to use their large muscles, to "run off steam," and to skip, shout, and jump where there is less chance of bumping into people and things. But this is only the beginning of the benefits of outdoor play. Teachers can take advantage of the outdoors to create many exciting learning experiences.

Many indoor activities can be brought outdoors, where the children can have an opportunity to use familiar materials in a new setting:

If the playground is near the classroom, take out clay and paints. Outdoors, the clay dries more quickly and must be worked with differently. Painting outside on a sunny day gives the children new experiences with light and color.

Have a picnic, either lunch or a snack, outdoors on a large blanket. This is a welcome change.

Move the woodworking table outdoors. The children will have more room to work, and the noise will disturb others less.

Read a book outdoors to an individual child or a small group of children. Books that deal with the outdoors—the wind, birds, trees, cars,

Reading a story in the playground makes a link between the indoors and the outdoors. It also provides structure for children who may need it.

etc.—are especially successful, as the setting often provides built-in props.

Use the tape recorder outside to record outdoor sounds.

Fill a tub for water play and provide a chance for blowing bubbles.

Take gerbils, guinea pigs, and hamsters outside so that the children can observe any changes in their behavior.

Take the record player outdoors for listening or dancing. Musical instruments are also fun outdoors. The children will notice a difference in the sound produced outside.

The children can participate in different art activities. They can:

Paint on oversized pieces of paper.

Paint large cardboard boxes. These can be used in a variety of ways in dramatic play.

Use large housepainting brushes with water or paint. Watching the water disappear is an interesting scientific experience.

Use found objects—pebbles, rocks, or leaves—as additions to, or imprints in, dough or clay.

Make rubbings of different surfaces.

Do tie dyeing and hang the finished work on a line.

Use colored chalks on the ground or the walls.

Trace shadows on large pieces of paper.

The teacher should take advantage of the changing seasons. In warm weather the children can:

Fill cups of water with liquid soap to make lots of bubbles. Outdoors, you don't have to worry about soap getting on the floor.

Wash dolls and furniture.

Play with a hose or sprinkler. (The children should bring a change of clothing.)

Finger-paint and use a hose for clean-up.

Plant and care for a garden.

Collect bugs and worms and let them go after everyone has had a chance to look at them. Don't forget the magnifying glass.

In cold weather the children can:

Make imprints in the snow with their bodies or with their hands or feet

Take out a bucket or a small container of water and watch what happens

Make snow figures

Throw snowballs (at a tree or wall)

Go sledding on large trays or pieces of cardboard

Look at snowflakes under a magnifying glass to see the different shapes

In fair weather the children can:

Collect and sort stones

Watch cloud patterns

Fill basins with sand and experiment with both wet and dry sand
Investigate the wind with pinwheels, streamers, and balloons

Outdoor activities that involve use of the large muscles include:

Climbing on jungle gyms and sturdy structures made from hollow blocks
Riding on large wheeled toys
Pushing, pulling, and lifting toys and hollow blocks and walking on boards
Twirling hoops around their waists or jumping in and out of hoops on the ground
Tugging ropes
Playing ball—throwing, catching, bouncing, and rolling
Jumping rope
Building large structures with hollow blocks
Walking across a balance beam or large log

The teacher's role outdoors is similar to her role in the classroom. Outdoor activities need careful and intelligent supervision to enrich children's ideas, enhance their individuality, and ensure their safety. The main points to remember are:

Be involved with the children.
Use everyday opportunities to further the children's development. A child may be able to climb higher on the jungle gym when he knows you are watching.
Ask questions that will help the children put their experiences into words, for example, "Do you remember what you did to get up so high?" or "What did you do to get started on the swing?"
Talk to the children about what they are doing; use words that describe their physical activities.
Establish rules with the children that are for their protection.
Prevent dangerous situations. Put a rubber mat under climbing equipment *before* anyone gets hurt.
Position yourself so that you can see everything that is going on and can step into a potentially hazardous situation.
Dress warmly so that you will feel comfortable when you are outdoors with the children during the winter months.
If you are uncomfortable when the children climb and are fearful that they might fall and hurt themselves, discuss your feelings with the cooperating teacher. She might suggest that you observe the children climbing to familiarize yourself with their abilities. She can also tell you what she has observed about individual children's physical abilities. Information like this will help you deal with your fears so that you can be more supportive of the children's efforts.

Making thoughtful comments to children helps them understand their physical experiences.

Some general suggestions include:

Limit the children's activities so that you and another adult or adults can effectively supervise their play. You might have one adult responsible for each activity area, such as woodworking, climbing, block building, and sand play.

Have a balance of activities. The children need to have the same choice of individual or group activities and active or quiet play that they have indoors.

Have both structured and unstructured activities. The children will enjoy playing on a slide as well as building structures with hollow blocks that they can use in a variety of dramatic-play activities.

Basic equipment The best outdoor equipment is safe, sturdy, and adaptable for many uses. You may want to provide the following:

Balancing equipment made from wooden boards 4 to 12 inches high raised on sawhorses of different heights. These boards can be used as slides or balance beams, and they can be changed frequently to create new possibilities.

Tires for swings, jumping, balancing, and rolling.

Simple props expand a child's dramatic play.

Hollow blocks. These are expensive, but they provide children with an opportunity to build a structure quickly and thus are especially good for use in dramatic-play activities. Because they are able to lift and carry these large blocks, using them gives children a feeling of competence.

Used cable wheels from telephone and electric companies make excellent climbing surfaces and can also be used for tables.

Large cardboard cartons. These can be used to make things or to play in.

Climbing equipment, such as a ladder box or a simple jungle gym that can be changed by adding walking boards to its sides.

A sandbox that is kept covered when not in use. In the sandbox you need sieves, pails, shovels, and unbreakable containers of various sizes.

Wheeled toys and wagons to carry things in or to pull and push.

FURTHER READINGS

Curriculum

Brown, Mary, and Norman Precious: *The Integrated Day in the Primary School*, Agathon Press, New York, 1969.
Pitcher, E. G., and M. Lasher, S. Fanburg, and L. Braun: *Helping Young Children Learn*, Merrill, Columbus, Ohio, 1974.
Sargent, Betsye: *The Integrated Day in the American School*, National Association of Independent Schools, Boston, 1970.

Language Arts

Arbuthnot, M. H.: *Children and Books*, Scott, Foresman, Chicago, 1957.
Gans, R.: *Common Sense in Teaching Reading*, Bobbs-Merrill, Indianapolis, 1963.
Smith, N. B., and R. Strickland: *Some Approaches to Reading*, Association for Childhood Education International, Washington, 1969.
Vygotsky, Lev: *Thought and Language*, M.I.T., Cambridge, Mass., 1967.

Mathematics

Hawkins, David: "I-Thou-It," *Mathematical Teaching*, no. 46, Association of Teachers of Mathematics,
Nuffield Foundation Booklets, Wiley, New York, Spring 1969. (Among those recommended are *I Do, I Understand, Beginning Shape and Size*, and *Pictorial Representation*.) (Available free from Early Childhood Education Study, 55 Chapel Street, Newton, Mass. 02160.)

Science

Hawkins, David: "Messing About in Science," *Science & Children*, vol. 2, no. 5, February 1965; *EST Quarterly Report*, vol. 3, no. 3, Summer–Fall 1965.

Lawrence, E., N. Isaacs, and W. Ramson: *Approaches to Science in the Primary School*, Educational Supply Association.

Navarra, J. G.: *The Development of Scientific Concepts in a Young Child*, Teachers College, New York, 1955.

Social Studies

Hanna, Sabaroff, Davies, and Farrar: *Geography in the Teaching of Social Studies Concepts and Skills*, Houghton Mifflin, Boston, 1966.

King, Ethel W., and August Kerber: *The Sociology of Early Childhood Education*, American Book, New York, 1968.

Art

Lowenfeld, Victor: *Creative and Mental Growth*, Macmillan, New York, 1957.

Montgomery, Chandler: *Art for Teachers of Children*, Merrill, Columbus, Ohio, 1968.

Pile, Naomi F.: *Art Experience for Young Children*, Macmillan, New York, 1973.

Music

Jacobs, E. Frances: *Finger Plays and Action Rhymes*, Lothrop, New York, 1941.

Seeger, Ruth Crawford: *American Folk Songs for Children in Homes, Schools and Nursery Schools*, Doubleday, Garden City, N.Y., 1948.

Sheehy, Emma D.: *Children Discover Music and Dance*, Holt, New York, 1963.

Stecher, Miriam: *Music and Movement Improvisations*, Macmillan, New York, 1972.

7 EXPANDING THE CURRICULUM

THE INTEGRATED CURRICULUM IN ACTION

The seven different curriculum areas have been described separately in order to highlight the specific skills and learning in each area. Yet children do not experience them as self-contained, separate packages. They don't just have reading, then math, and so on, in an integrated curriculum. All the curriculum areas are combined in a variety of daily experiences.

Building with blocks, taking trips, doing woodworking, and cooking are some of the ongoing activities that encompass all areas of the curriculum and provide opportunities for growth in all areas of children's development.

BLOCKS

Blocks are a vital part of the learning environment. They are an excellent medium for helping the teacher further understand the integrated curriculum and how this approach meets the needs of the whole child.

Look at the many shapes blocks come in. Think of all the possible forms you can create even with one simple shape. There is no one way of using blocks—no right or wrong way, and no good or bad way. Each child can select his or her own problem and then try to solve it: "Can I make a bridge?" "Can I make a tunnel?" "Can I make a solid floor?" "Can I repeat my own design?" As children work with blocks, they go through the three stages of the creative process. (See "Children's Art: The Creative Process" in Chapter 6, The Curriculum.) The teacher never builds; she encourages the children and ensures their safety. Children need a very large supply of blocks and a big, free area in which to work. This has been discussed under "Room Arrangement" in Chapter 4, The Classroom.

Why are blocks stressed so much by teachers of early childhood classrooms? What is their value? Let's look at this activity first from the point of view of the whole child.

Physical benefits The child starts with simple building, which develops gross motor coordination. When his building becomes more complicated and more representational, he uses fine motor coordination to place a block, a car, or a boat in the proper place. All this requires delicate eye-hand coordination.

Social benefits Most children tend to work with blocks almost as a team. One child starts, and another joins. They make suggestions to one another, discuss possibilities, and feel good about sharing a positive experience. They also feel good about working out disagreements.

Block play strengthens perceptual learning such as eye-hand coordination, directionality, and measurement of space.

Emotional benefits Watch a child step back and look at what she has done to create a three-dimensional world of her own. She can also crash this world and harm no one. The satisfaction, the sense of accomplishment, and the feeling of self-worth are vital to the child. Her friends admire her work too, and this makes her feel important.

Intellectual benefits The child solves the problems he has set for himself. He tries a block and changes it for another, and he discusses his concerns with his friends. He is engaged in learning in all curriculum areas.

Relation of Blocks to the Curriculum Areas

Language arts Listen as the children build. There is an almost constant flow of language. Important words are used, such as *big*, *taller*, *more than*, *less than*, *over*, *under*, and *on top of.*

Mathematics Blocks are mathematically scaled. The unit block is exactly one-half the size of the double-unit block; two double-unit blocks or four unit blocks equal one quadruple-unit block; two triangles equal one unit block; etc. (See Figure 4-1 for other mathematical relationships.) Children count blocks not only one by one but also in sets. "Here are two blocks," "Here are four," etc. They are also using the language of mathematics.

Social studies As they use blocks, the children's world is re-created and then understood. They build neighborhoods, airports, garages, roads, and cities. There is a considerable amount of dramatic play in the block area. The children play out many roles as they begin to understand their own role in this complex world.

Science The children construct buildings, bridges, and arches. They build ramps of different heights and lengths to see how this affects the speed at which a car travels down a ramp.

Art Blocks are a creative art medium. The child is making a three-dimensional art form; he is creating a world.

Music As the child bends to pick up a block and put it in place, there is rhythmical body movement. As he moves around his structure, adding to it and changing it, he swings so as not to destroy what he has made. He moves his body carefully in a space that he is aware of. He hears the various sounds the blocks make as they clank and fall, and he recognizes the differences in the sounds. He frequently develops a rhythmical chant, and his friends join in. A child may push three blocks along the floor and chant a "choo-choo" song that he makes up as he plays.

The Teacher's Role

The teacher is ready to make suggestions or supply enriching materials whenever necessary. If the children have built a waterfront, she might suggest making a finger painting of water to put under the bridge. If they have made a train, she might supply a hole punch and suggest that they make tickets and then punch them.

Block play is vital for the development of the whole child. The teacher needs to be sensitive to the integrated-curriculum concept and supply the necessary materials whenever she feels this will enrich the children's play and not interfere with their own ideas.

TRIPS FOR YOUNG CHILDREN

Trips are:

> A shared experience
> A firsthand encounter
> A way to acquire new information
> A way to correct misconceptions
> A way to directly reinforce what is already known

Every trip should be:

> Related to the children's age and interests
> Purposeful
> Planned
> *Fun*
> Followed up with classroom discussions, activities, and experiences

For the Children

Before the trip

They should be prepared   The children need to be part of the planning for the trip. They need to know where they are going and why, how they are going there, and how long the trip will last (until lunch or all day, for example). They should know whether there is anything they are supposed to bring.

They should know the focus of the trip   The children should know what the purpose of the trip is and whether they will be looking at something specific or exploring everything.

They should know the rules   The children need to know what is expected of them—for example, that they are to walk two by two or in small groups with an adult, that they must hold hands when crossing a street, that they must stay seated while riding in a vehicle, or that they will wear name tags.

During the trip

They can enjoy getting there and back   Going to and from the destination is an important part of the trip. The children need to be able to talk and sing when this doesn't conflict with the safety rules.

They can ask questions, explore, and discover   You must allow ample time for them to see what there is to see. When it is appropriate, they need to move around and talk with one another and with the adults.

After the trip

They can talk about the experience   The children should be encouraged to discuss the trip in small and large groups.

They can build on the experience   The children need to incorporate their new information into dramatic play, block building, and other forms of creative work. They can also dictate simple stories to the teacher. You would be wise to avoid asking the children to draw something specific that they saw; you should respect their individuality by having them draw the things that interested them.

For the Teacher

Before the trip

Visit the destination yourself   You should do this to establish:

> Traveling time
> Traveling directions
> Location of information booths
> Location of bathrooms (and whether they require money)
> Location of telephones
> Location of eating areas and water fountains
> Location of rest areas
> What the main points of interest are
> How much time will be required to see what you want to see

Prepare a travel kit   This should include Band-Aids, first-aid cream, tissues, paper and plastic bags, and extra money.

Get permission slips from parents

Make arrangements for food for the trip   Even if the trip is short, you will probably want to bring a snack. If you are providing lunch, it is also a good idea to make sure there are extras. Snacks are also necessary for the trip back, when the children are tired.

Make name tags   These need to be durable and covered in either clear Contact or other plastic coating. Be sure that they can be attached securely.

Inviting parents on a trip ensures a more comfortable, informal experience and makes discussions at home more meaningful.

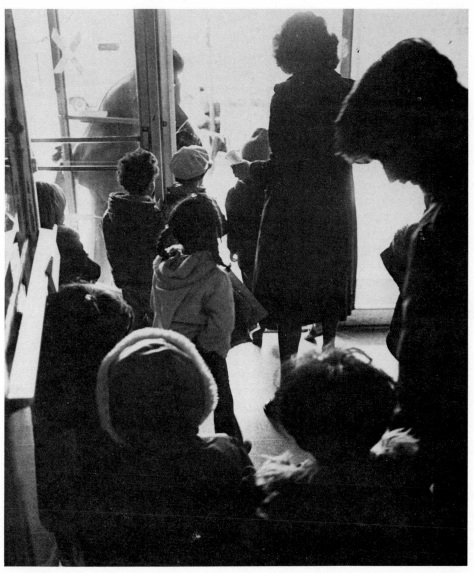

Make sure there will be enough adults on the trip   Get in touch with the parents and invite them to come along.

Make travel arrangements

During the trip   While you are taking the trip, you should:

Help the children remember the focus of the trip (without cutting off other interests).
Ask stimulating and open-ended questions, questions like "Why do you think . . .?
Listen to the children.
Provide information.
Take pictures (if possible).
Avoid trying to see or do too much.
Keep track of all the children. It is often helpful to break the group up into smaller subgroups, each with a responsible adult.
You should take occasional head counts.
Show your own enjoyment and excitement.
Make the trip an enjoyable experience for the children.
Be sensitive to the children's fatigue and overstimulation.
Provide enough rest periods and food.
Provide enough structure to make the trip safe, while playing down the rules and playing up the *fun.*

After the trip   Encourage the children to talk about their experience. In spontaneous and planned discussions, you need to:

Help the children remember the highlights
Recall the focus of the trip.
Go over the trip's sequence: "What did we do first?" "Then what did we do?"

You can record these discussions on tape.
After the trip you can also:

Write about the trip with the children. You can write down everything the children say or cover just the main points.
Make a book about the experience. Using the photographs and the children's comments, you and the children can make a book to keep in the library area. The children will then have their own records of their trips, and they can refer back to these books throughout the year.
Sing about the trip. Find songs that relate to the trip or help the children make up their own. (The tune from "The Wheels on the Bus" lends itself to improvisation.)
Use the shared experience. It can help enrich dramatic play and block building.

Bring in materials that will add to the children's reenactment and representation of their experience.

Find books and stories that relate to the trip.

Some of these follow-up activities, like discussions, are essential if the children are to get the most out of the experience. Other activities depend on the children's interest and on the available resources

Some Additional Suggestions for Taking Trips

1 Some children may evidence separation anxiety before and during a trip. They may ask, "Will Mommy know where I am?" Some less verbal children may cry or become irritable and restless for no apparent reason. The wise teacher recognizes that this may be a result of separation anxiety. It is advisable to take a few short neighborhood walks first. You should refer to these walks as "trips." This helps the children to see that they go on a trip and then return. In some instances it may be necessary to have a child accompanied by someone from home.

2 For a child who may present problems on a trip, it may be helpful to first take him on a short walk alone. Then, when this child is ready to join a small group, it may be necessary to have one adult responsible primarily for keeping an eye on him.

3 Don't forget the familiar. Children enjoy informal excursions to the supermarket, the laundromat, etc. You can always help the children to see these places in a new way.

Some Ideas for Taking Trips in the Community

1 Take a "collecting" walk around your neighborhood with small groups of children; this is a way of finding items that will add to your program and help the children become more aware of the world around them. The children, provided with shopping bags, can gather a variety of items: leaves, rocks, twigs, feathers, shells, etc.

2 Carefully check your community, and you might discover:

A bakery that will allow small groups of children to visit and watch cake and bread being made

A lumberyard that will allow the children to watch large pieces of wood being sawed

A veterinarian with puppies or kittens in his care who might talk to the children about them

A fish store that has a live tank with lobsters and crabs for viewing

3 The firehouse and the police station are good places to visit, but you must make an appointment first. Most local libraries have storytelling hours and welcome preschool classes. It is a good idea to check with the librarian about the story that is planned for the day you will be visiting, as the children may need some preparation.

4   If you are fortunate enough to have a senior citizens' center in your community, check to see whether your class could attend a concert or an art show presented by the older adults. One school formed a very meaningful relationship with a senior citizens' group, who returned their visit and instituted a storytelling program within the preschool classroom.

WOODWORKING

Working with wood provides young children with a splendid opportunity for growth—physically, emotionally, intellectually, and socially. Working with tools requires accuracy, eye-hand coordination, and the use of the small and large muscles. Tools are real and provide children with an opportunity to experience success with materials that adults use. For young children this is extremely important—they have little control over their lives, often having to wait for adults to do things for them. Using a hammer or saw enables them to experience themselves as effective, powerful people. Woodworking is a noisy activity, and it provides children with an excellent "legitimate" way to create noise—to sound off and to feel, hear, and see their own strength, as they pound a nail or saw a piece of wood in half.

Working with wood offers children opportunities in many curriculum areas.

Mathematics   Woodworking provides practice in measuring length and width. For example, the child must check to make certain that he has a nail of the right length for his piece of wood.

Science   The children have an opportunity to observe different types of wood, such as maple and pine. They can ask questions like, "What happens to wood when it is wet?" "What happens to wood when it is sawed?"

Social studies   The children can name things that are made of wood in the classroom and at home. In one class, several children were investigating different types of wood; they asked the other children in the class to find out what kind of wood their kitchen chairs were made of. This investigation led them, with the aid of the teacher, to make several trips to a museum; there they saw chairs that were made over 100 years ago, and they tried to find out whether maple was as popular then as it is now.

Language arts   Woodworking provides young children with a new, rich vocabulary; they learn words related to using tools, (*hammer, saw, vise, nails, screw, hasp, clamp, tape measure*), words describing the various wood surfaces (*smooth, rough, soft, thick*), and the names of trees (*maple, redwood, pine*).

Children working with wood relate to one another; often they help one another and, above all, speak to one another. They discuss their work and their plans for what they are making. They describe to one another what they are doing. Sometimes children who have been blockbuilding together need a particular item, such as a boat or a truck, which is not included in the block accessories. Going to the workbench and making the item they need to complete their play gives them a sense of themselves as effective people. During woodworking, an idea is thought about, planned for, created, and used. This provides an excellent opportunity for the teacher to talk with the children about their achievement.

Music Woodworking is certainly related to sound production. The children have the opportunity to listen to many sounds—the sound of different hammers against different kinds of woods and the sound of the saw and the drill. Using tools requires moving the body in rhythm. The rhythm changes for each activity, such as hammering and sawing. A group of children who were trying to saw a difficult piece of wood started singing spontaneously, "Michael, Saw the Wooden Board, Hallelujah" (to the tune of "Michael, Row the Boat Ashore"). The teacher joined in, and they discovered that singing helped the work move along. This incident led the class to an inquiry into many other work songs, such as, "John Henry," "Take This Hammer," and "The Volga Boatman," trying them out as they did various difficult jobs in the room.

Art Constructing with wood involves many of the creative aspects of art. Selecting the right piece of wood, placing it correctly to make your design, and working with it to produce your own creation—all this is part of the woodworking experience and helps give children a greater awareness of themselves and a chance to clarify their own identities.

Physical education Woodworking provides children with an opportunity to develop physical skills and a chance to see their own growth as they develop more accuracy in the use of tools. You can save some of the woodwork a child completes over the year. Periodically, you and the child can look at the work and, together, see the kind of progress the child has made, such as sawing wood evenly and hammering nails in a straight line.

As in all activities, you must be sensitive to the children's individual styles of working with wood. Some will be hesitant, fearful, and relunctant; others will be exuberant, excited, and aggressive; and still others will be calm, careful, cautious, and unrelenting. The information obtained from observing the way individual children work can be very valuable to you in planning for their future needs. You must evaluate who needs help and how much help should be offered. Generally, careful observation will tell you when to help. When a child looks frustrated and has been working at a task for some time, you can ask whether your help is needed. Often, clarifying the problem by asking, for example, "Why do you think the wood isn't holding?" or "Have you tried holding the saw like this?" is enough to enable the child to finish the work. If a child has struggled with a piece of work and finally achieves what he set out to do, it is valuable to express your understanding of the problems he faced and also to restate the solutions he found. You should also check the woodworking materials. Is the wood too thick for the size nails you have provided? Are the hammers and saws in good working order? Did plywood or some other inappropriate wood get mixed into the woodpile?

Sometimes children choose to do an impossible project. They decide to construct something that just won't work. Here, you need to help them clarify their thinking and approach the problem more realistically. You must also be able to help the children compromise their ideas and to decide on something that will give them a feeling of accomplishment.

At the Workbench

Not more than two or three children should be at the workbench at one time. They need room for safety and for their own comfort.

You should be present in the woodworking area to supervise the situation, and you should be especially sensitive to the individual needs of the children working with wood. Some children require more attention than others, and it might be necessary to limit the number of such children engaged in this activity at one time.

Regardless of their age, children need time to develop skills and ability in the use of woodworking tools. The three-year-old is interested in hammering and sawing as an activity, not in creating a finished product.

Once children have successfully hammered nails into wood, they keep repeating and repeating the process without anything special in mind. Sawing a piece of wood in half might be all the work some children will do. They are not sawing the wood in order to make something specific with it. It is the act of sawing itself that is important to them. As children mature, they start creating something that has a specific meaning for them (see page 152). Five-year-olds construct boats, cars, houses, or abstract objects that are artistically pleasing. Often they make things that they can use in play. This is one of the many advantages of working with a material as solid as wood. Five- and six-year-olds who have had a lot of experience with wood measure and draw lines when they are sawing. They are able to plan their projects beforehand. It is important to note that older children who have had no experience with woodworking need time to explore the materials and to hammer and saw for the "sake of hammering and sawing" before they really construct anything.

Materials

A woodworking table might be an expensive addition for a classroom with a limited budget. As an alternative, you can attach C-clamps, which are far less expensive, to an old wooden table with the legs sawed off to a height of 24 inches; this is an excellent surface for woodworking. You will also need the following equipment:

    Claw hammers weighing about 11 to 13 ounces.
    Slender wire nails with flat heads and sharp points, ³/₄ inch, 1 inch, and 1¹/₄ inches long.
    Crosscut saws, 12 to 16 inches long.

A teacher may have to help by steadying a difficult tool but should never do the work.

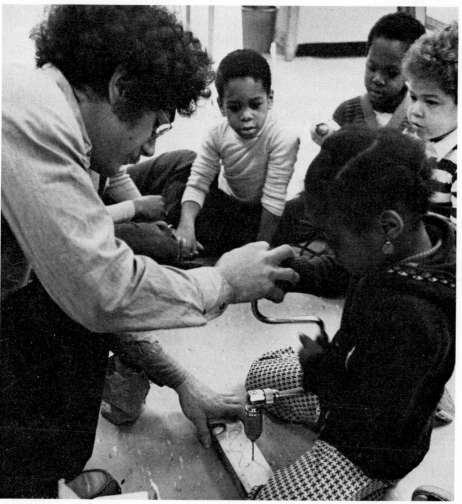

An auger or brace for boring holes. This tool is difficult for children under five to use and requires the teacher's assistance.

Sandpaper. Several different qualities should be provided. Paper that is too fine takes too long to use and should be avoided.

Screws and screwdrivers should not be offered. Screwdrivers slip, require a great deal of pressure, and are dangerous for young children.

Proper storage of tools is important to the woodworking activity. The teacher and the children should treat the tools with respect and handle them with care. For easy storage it is helpful to provide a hanging pegboard, with the outline of the tools marked on it. (See "Room Arrangement" in Chapter 4, The Classroom.) Children feel secure when they know where things belong and where they can find what they need. Nails and accessories can be stored in clear boxes in the table drawer or on a nearby shelf. Wood can be stored in a box or basket near the woodworking table. It is often helpful to have separate boxes for small and large pieces of wood. Parents and teachers who establish a friendly relationship with the people at the neighborhood lumberyard will find they are willing to put aside a weekly supply for the class. Lumberyards will also save sawdust for schools (sawdust, mixed with wheat paste and water, makes an interesting modeling material for children). A bucket can be placed under the woodworking table to catch the sawdust when the children saw, enabling them to see the sawdust collect firsthand.

When first introducing woodworking, it is advisable to buy some precut pine boards from the lumberyard so that the children can experience as much success as possible with the material when they are in the exploratory stage. It is suggested that pieces be cut 2 to 3 feet long and 1 to 2 inches thick. Pine dowels are an important addition to the workbench. Dowels may be used to create smokestacks, axles, and towers, and they are necessary for work with the auger. Soft wood, such as pine, poplar, and cedar, is easier to work with than harder wood. Plywood should be avoided; it splinters easily. Wood that is too soft, such as balsa, will also splinter.

After the children have had some experience with hammering and sawing, accessories can be introduced to the woodworking area to add interest and excitement. Such items would include rubber bands, jar covers, string, bottle caps, and paper-towel tubing and glue.

Helpful Tips

Hammer To start a child hammering, have him hold the nail upright with one hand; tell him to hold the hammer in the other hand and to give short, light taps. Once the nail has pierced the wood and is holding, have the child remove his hand from the nail. This hand can now be placed on the table while the child swings the hammer to pound the nail all the

A child can get the nail started successfully if the nail has a large head, the hammer is the right size, and the wood is soft.

way in. Children will find their own ways of swinging a hammer. At first they tend to grab it near the head to gain control. As they learn to control it, they will hold it closer to the end to gain greater leverage. Children can learn how to remove a nail by inserting the claw of the hammer under the nail and rocking it back and forth until the nail comes loose.

Saw   Draw a line down the board you wish to cut. Help the child saw on the outside of the line. Check to see that the vise or C-clamp is tightly in place. The child should stand with one foot forward so that his weight can be shifted from one foot to the other. This also gives the child freedom to move more comfortably. When the child starts to saw, he can set the saw alongside the pencil mark and pull back gradually. This may be repeated several times until the saw stays in the started notch, or the "kerf." When this happens, the child can proceed to saw downward, holding the saw at a 45-degree angle. Children often try to press down as they saw. This causes the saw to catch. A saw works on friction, not force. Children need to be helped just to move the saw, not press it.

Sandpaper It is easier to use sandpaper if it securely thumbtacked around a small block of wood. This gives the child a sturdier surface to work with.

Although many educators agree that woodworking provides young children with an excellent firsthand learning experience, very few preschool classrooms actually include woodworking in their programs. Perhaps the current change in attitudes toward women's role in society will encourage teachers to include this important material in their programs. Since teachers in most early childhood classrooms have traditionally been women and since society has frowned upon women in "unladylike" situations, teachers have been reluctant and often afraid to use woodworking tools in the classroom. It is hoped that as attitudes change and as more information becomes available, woodworking will take its rightful place in the preschool environment.

COOKING

There is a tremendous amount of learning involved in cooking, besides the fun of making something and eating it. The task of following directions—presented orally or in writing, with a prescribed sequence of steps—is a helpful, structured activity for children to be engaged in. Cooking requires good eye-hand coordination. This is developed while using the utensils for mixing, pouring, slicing, chopping, peeling, etc. The task can be geared to the children's abilities in order to assure their success and yet give them practice at the same time. The adventure of seeing, feeling, tasting, and smelling makes use of their senses in a very real way, giving them the kind of feedback that words cannot. Not only do they learn the characteristics of the ingredients, but they also begin to understand numbers and fractions as a result of actually measuring the quantities. Children learn by doing, and cooking provides maximum participation in the process.

Cooking in school offers children an opportunity to try out adult roles and create something real, with real tools and real food. Parents can then be encouraged to let their children participate in food preparation at home.

Food is basic to life itself, and food and eating are often surrounded by strong emotions. Often children develop a great concern for the

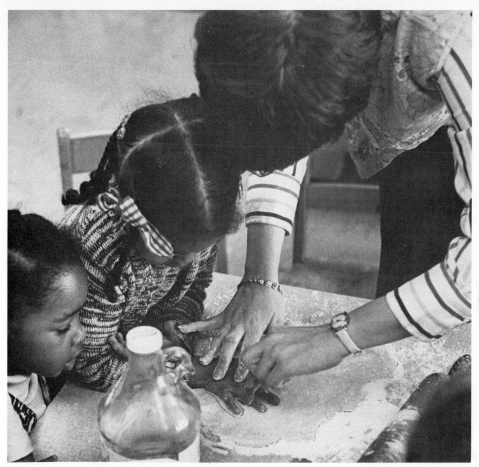

"Hand cookies" are good to eat, make the cooking experience personal, and provide learning in all areas.

availability of food and equate food with love and security. Some children may need to gorge themselves for a while until they feel comfortable in this cooking situation. Becoming active in preparing food will be helpful to such children.

Language arts, science, mathematics, and social studies are aided by cooking activities: keeping track of the time, seeing changes occur, learning new words related to cooking, following directions in a certain sequence, getting ideas from books, discovering where various foods come from, learning about the food preferences of different ethnic groups, working together as a team, and sharing food with friends. The learning possibilities are tremendous. Cooking in school is a cumulative process, starting with very simple steps and going to more complex ones.

1   Think through the entire cooking process before you start. If you have never used this particular recipe before, try it out by yourself first.
2   Make certain that all the utensils are in good working order and that you have all the necessary ingredients.
3   Maintain strict supervision around the stove, knives, etc.
4   Have a definite place for the utensils so that they can be quickly put back for easy clean-up. Knowing where things belong gives children a sense of security.
5   Halve fruits and vegetables that might slip or roll when chopped.
6   Use extra-large bowls and pans to prevent spillovers.
7   Keep the size of the cooking group small so that cooking can be a relaxed, meaningful experience.
8   Have extra ingredients to allow for tastes and spills.
9   Allow plenty of time for the experience.
10 Use semisharp knives with serrated edges; dull knives slip and cause injury.
11 Use as many hand-powered tools as possible (e.g., eggbeaters rather than electric mixers) so that the children are actually doing the work.
12 Make clean-up a part of the ongoing cooking process.
13 In the beginning of the cooking curriculum, make the experience truly individual so that the children can complete the process independently. For this, you need four to six sets of everything: bowls, measuring spoons, etc.

Beginning Experiences

The first cooking experience should be the easiest kind: a one- or two-process activity which does not include dangerous steps using heat or difficult implements. Consider making chocolate milk or lemonade as a starter. For each of these, the children can make their own individual recipes by deciding how much sugar to use in lemonade and how much chocolate powder to put in chocolate milk.

For chocolate milk, you need several containers of milk (depending on the number of children involved), a large box of Quik or a similar product, a measuring cup, and a teaspoon. You may also provide each child with a piece of construction paper, some cutout spoon shapes made of sturdy paper, and a cutout cup shape (Figure 7-1a). These can be pasted on the construction paper to show the exact number of teaspoons of chocolate powder used to make that particular child's drink. It would look like Figure 7-1b.

For lemonade the same procedure may be used. Added to this would

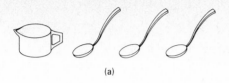

(a)

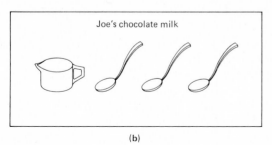

(b)

Figure 7-1
Chocolate milk.

be squeezing the lemons, looking at the inside of the fruit, counting the seeds, and adding water and as many spoonsful of sugar as the child needs.

The child's recipe might look like Figure 7-2 (page 198).

Each recipe will be different, depending on each child's taste. This experience also helps the children to be aware of individual differences.

Some More Cooking Experiences

ORANGE JUICE

Equipment	*Ingredients*
Hand orange-juice squeezer	Oranges
Small strainer	
Cups	
Knife	
Measuring cup	

Steps
1 Cut the oranges in half.
2 Smell the oranges, look at their texture, and look for seeds.
3 Place each orange half on the squeezer, press, and squeeze.
4 Pour the juice through the strainer into the measuring cup to see how much there is.
5 Look at the pulp.
6 Count the seeds.
7 Drink the juice.

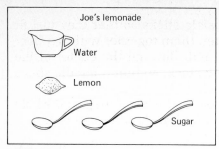

Figure 7-2
Lemonade.

It would be interesting, after this experience has been repeated, to offer the children canned and frozen juice so that they can compare them. A chart could be made to show which children in the group favor which kind of juice. The same procedure could be used with grapefruit.

It would also be interesting to look at the various types of oranges. Some are truly "juice oranges," and some are for eating. The amount of juice squeezed from the various kinds of oranges could be compared. The taste, color, and number of seeds could be recorded.

Fresh butter   You can make butter by beating cream with an eggbeater, but it's fun to make your own butter churn. You need a 1-pint jar with a screw top, two flat popsicle sticks, scissors, a rubber band, a round stick the size of a pencil, a hammer, and nails (Figure 7-3a). Five-year-olds can make a butter churn with help.

Figure 7-3
(a) Equipment needed for making a butter churn. (b) Completed churn.

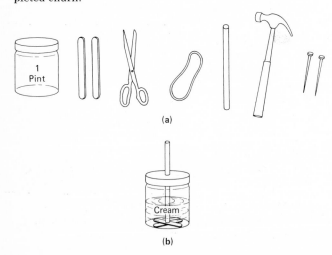

First, make the dasher. Cut the popsicle sticks so that they just fit into the bottom of the jar, lying flat. Fasten them together with a rubber band into an X shape. Hammer a small nail through the center of the popsicle sticks into the bottom of the long stock, so that a handle sticks straight up from the X.

Next, use a large nail to hammer a hole in the top of the jar; the hole should be big enough for the stick to go through. Pull the nail out.

Pour $1/2$ pint of heavy cream into the jar.

Put the dasher in the jar and tightly screw on the top so that the stick comes through the hole (Figure 7-3b).

Now your're ready to churn. Move the dasher up and down very fast. After awhile the cream will get very thick, and you will have whipped cream; keep on churning, and soon lumps of butter will appear. The lumps will get bigger until all the butter is separated out. (The liquid left in the jar is buttermilk.) Put the butter in a bowl and pour a little ice water on it. Press the water through the butter with a wooden spoon. The water will turn white. Pour off the liquid. Mix a little salt (if you like) into the butter. Spread it on bread or crackers and *enjoy*!

CREAM CHEESE BALLS

Equipment	*Ingredients*
Knife	One-quarter of a package of cream
Bowl	cheese
Spoon for mixing	$1/2$ cup and 2 tablespoons
Measuring cup	powdered sugar
Teaspoon	Drop of vanilla
Plates	Nuts, coconut, sprinkles, or
	cinnamon and sugar

Steps
1 Cut the piece of cream cheese.
2 Mix in the bowl until soft.
3 Pour the sugar into the bowl and mix.
4 Add the vanilla.
5 Roll the mixture into balls.
6 Roll the balls in the various toppings.

UNCOOKED CHOCOLATE PUDDING

Equipment	*Ingredients*
Juicer	3 tablespoons lemon juice (use half a large
Deep bowl	lemon)
Eggbeater	One can of evaporated milk ($5^{1}/_{3}$ ounces)
Spoon	$1/2$ cup presweetened cocoa mix (Quik or a
Cups and spoons	similar product)
for serving	

Steps
1 Squeeze the lemon.
2 Pour the evaporated milk into the bowl.
3 Pour the lemon juice into the milk and beat with the eggbeater.
4 When the mixture thickens, add the cocoa mix, a few spoonsful at a time.
5 Beat until the pudding is thick and creamy.

Serves four. Eat right away, or it can be frozen.

MIXED FRUIT PUDDING

Equipment	*Ingredients*
Knife	Two ripe bananas
Flat-bottomed bowl	$\frac{1}{2}$ cup applesauce
Potato masher	2 tablespoons honey
Wire wisk	Cinnamon
Cups or bowls for serving	
Spoons for eating	

Steps
1 Peel the bananas.
2 Cut them into small pieces.
3 Put the pieces in the bowl and mash them with the potato masher until smooth.
4 Stir in the applesauce, the peanut butter, and the honey.
5 Stir the mixture with the wire wisk until smooth.
6 Serve, topped with cinnamon.

Serves four.

FRUIT BARS

Equipment	*Ingredients*
Teaspoon	1 cup raisins
Food grinder	1 cup dates
Large bowl	1 cup dried apricots
Vegetable peeler	1 cup dried prunes
	$\frac{1}{2}$ cup nuts (any kind)
	Rind of one orange
	1 teaspoon ground ginger
	Grated coconut

Steps
1 To get the orange rind, shave off the thin orange part on the outside of the orange with the vegetable peeler.
2 Put the dried fruit, the nuts, and the orange rind through the food grinder.
3 Put all these ingredients in the bowl.
4 Add the ginger.

5 Mix well and shape into little balls.
6 Roll the balls into the grated coconut.

Makes four dozen.

ICE CREAM

Equipment	*Ingredients*
Clean coffee can	One egg
with plastic cover	$1/4$ cup honey
Plastic or wooden	1 cup milk
pail or ice bucket	$1/2$ cup heavy cream
Large spoon	1 teaspoon vanilla
	Ice
	Salt

Steps
1 Beat the egg and the honey in the coffee can.
2 Add the milk, the cream, the vanilla, and a dash of salt.
3 Put a layer of ice in the bottom of the pail. Crushed ice freezes smoother and faster, but cubes will work also. (If you are making this in the winter, you can also use snow.)
4 Sprinkle the ice with 1 tablespoon of salt.
5 Put the plastic cover over the coffee can and set the can on top of the ice. Pack more salt and ice in the pail around the sides of the can. When the ice is almost to the top of the can, remove the lid.
6 Stir the mixture around and around with the spoon, letting the can turn also.
7 Keep stirring and watching.
The children can take turns with this because it takes from 15 to 30 minutes for the cream to mush. You can eat it right away, while it's soft; it's like custard. If you put more ice and salt around the can, cover it, and let it sit for an hour, and it will harden.

"YOUR CHOICE" COOKIES (Baked or unbaked)

Equipment	*Ingredients*
Cookie sheet	One stick of butter or margarine
Bowl	3 cups of oatmeal
Measuring cup	1 cup honey
Measuring spoons	3 tablespoons powdered cocoa
Small pot	(unsweetened)
	$3/4$ cup powdered milk
	$1/2$ teaspoon salt
	2 teaspoons vanilla
	$1/2$ cup peanut butter
	$1/2$ cup raisins

Steps
1 Melt the butter over low heat or on a radiator.
2 Stir in the oatmeal and mix well.
3 Add all the other ingredients.
4 Mix well with your hands. The mixture will be very stiff.
5 Wash your hands.
6 Put a bowl of water on the table and use it to wet your hands before you shape the cookies.
7 Roll the dough into balls, "snakes", or any shape you like.

Either eat the cookies right away or put them on the cookie sheet (buttered), flatten them, and bake for 10 or 12 minutes in a 350° oven. It's interesting to fix half the dough for baking and the other half for eating right away.

Salads Salads involve cutting, scraping, peeling, chopping, tearing, mixing, shredding, and coring. Here are some things the children can do and think about when making salads:

Which are fruits and which are vegetables? (Sorting experience.)
Which things need to be peeled?
Which things need to be chopped, left whole, grated, or shredded?
What different parts of the plant do the fruits and vegetables come from?
Take out the seeds and compare them. Then plant them.
Eat the fruits and vegetables raw. At another time cook them and discuss the differences.
How should we serve the salad? Should we put it all in one bowl, or should we put the fruits and vegetables on separate plates and let everyone mix his or her own?
What things can we mix to make a dressing for the salad?
What other things can we put into the salad besides fruits and vegetables? (Some ideas: cheese, eggs, bacon, nuts, popcorn, and marshmallows.)

Vegetables can be eaten raw and served with a dip made of cheese, yogurt, or sour cream.
Don't forget celery, which can be stuffed with cream cheese, cottage cheese, or peanut butter. This is a good beginning cooking experience since it requires cutting the celery and spreading the filling into the crevice.

CARROT SALAD

Equipment	*Ingredients*
Large bowl	Five carrots
Measuring cup	1 cup raisins
Spoon	Juice from one lemon
	Honey

Steps

1 Scrub the carrots well, but leave the skins on. Grate them into the bowl.
2 Mix in the raisins.
3 Squeeze the lemon juice over the mixture.
4 Add honey to taste.

It's fun to make a salad and have each child bring in a different fruit or vegetable.

PEANUT BUTTER

Equipment	*Ingredients*
Food grinder or grain grinder	1 pound peanuts, roasted in the shells
Bowl	Salt
(An electric blender may be used, but this does not offer the children a real experience.)	Small amount of peanut oil

Steps
1 Crack open the shells.
2 Take out the peanuts and remove the brown skins.
3 Put the peanuts through the food grinder three times or more.
4 Add enough peanut oil to make a thick paste.
5 Add salt to taste.

Experiment with other nuts such as cashews, walnuts, or almonds. You can also compare homemade peanut butter with the kind bought in a store. Find out who likes which kind and make a chart of these preferences.

SKILLET COOKIES

Equipment	*Ingredients*
Large bowl	3 tablespoons soft butter
Measuring spoons	$1/2$ cup brown sugar
Measuring cup	1 cup unbleached white flour
Sifter	2 tablespoons powdered milk
Electric skillet	1 teaspoon cinnamon
	$1/4$ teaspoon salt
	$1/2$ cup wheat germ
	3 tablespoons honey
	$1/2$ cup raisins
	Butter for frying

Steps
1 Mix the butter and brown sugar together in the bowl.
2 Sift the flour, powdered milk, cinnamon, and salt into the bowl.
3 Add the wheat germ, honey, and raisins.

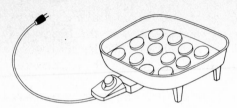

Figure 7-4
Making fried cookies.

4 Sprinkle some flour on a clean tabletop. Get some flour on your hands and then shape pieces of the dough into little balls.
5 Roll the balls around in the flour on the table and then flatten them out.
6 Heat the skillet to 300° and melt 1 tablespoon of butter in it.
7 Put in as many cookies as you can fit into the pan (Figure 7-4). Cook them until they start to puff up and are golden brown on the bottom (about five minutes).
8 Turn them over and cook them a minute or two.
9 Take them out and cool them.

CHEESY FROSTING

Equipment	*Ingredients*
Bowl	One 8-ounce package of cream cheese
Measuring cup	$1/4$ cup cocoa powder (unsweetened)
Measuring spoons	1 teaspoon vanilla
Spreaders	2 tablespoons honey
Knives or flat wooden ice-cream spoons	$1/4$ cup powdered milk (non-instant, nongrainy kind)

Steps
1 Let the cream cheese sit in the bowl until soft.
2 Mix in the cocoa powder.
3 Add the vanilla.
4 Stir in the honey.
5 Add powdered milk until the mixture is the right thickness.
6 Spread the frosting on a cake, cupcake, or cookies.

You can frost plain store-bought cookies if you can't bake your own.

Easy frosting Mix powdered sugar with a small amount of milk. The frosting should be thick enough to spread. Softened butter may be added, if desired.

The frosting can be flavored with vanilla flavoring, orange or lemon juice, almond extract, etc. The children can choose which flavoring they want and add it to the frosting.

You can add cocoa (and a few drops of vanilla) to make chocolate frosting, or you can add a few drops of food coloring to the frosting—pink, green, etc. Here, again, the children can choose. While the frosting is still sticky, you can sprinkle many things on top, such as coconut, sprinkles, raisins, or chocolate bits.

Some recipes lend themselves to large picture charts that are easy for the children to follow themselves. Two examples are French toast (Figure 7-5) and vegetable soup (Figure 7-6).

One Cooking Experience

Every cooking activity involves a variety of learning experiences. A group of nursery school children had the following experiences when

Figure 7-5
Recipe for French toast.

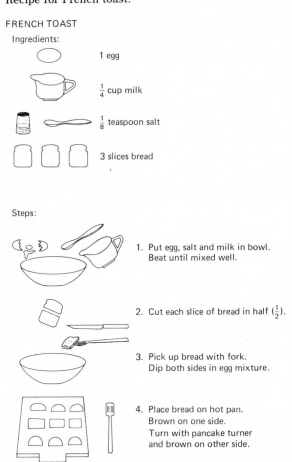

FRENCH TOAST

Ingredients:

1 egg

$\frac{1}{4}$ cup milk

$\frac{1}{8}$ teaspoon salt

3 slices bread

Steps:

1. Put egg, salt and milk in bowl.
   Beat until mixed well.

2. Cut each slice of bread in half ($\frac{1}{2}$).

3. Pick up bread with fork.
   Dip both sides in egg mixture.

4. Place bread on hot pan.
   Brown on one side.
   Turn with pancake turner
   and brown on other side.

VEGETABLE SOUP

Ingredients:

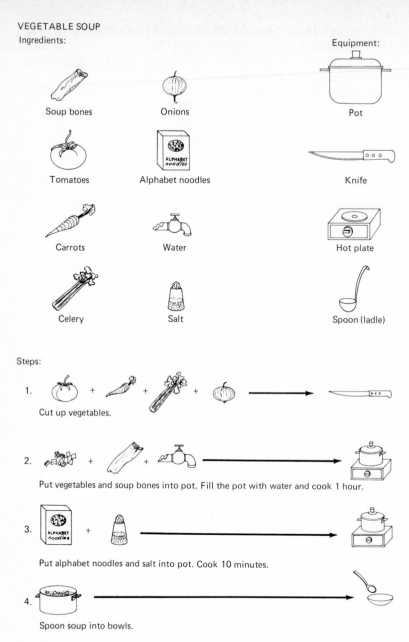

Equipment:

Soup bones   Onions   Pot

Tomatoes   Alphabet noodles   Knife

Carrots   Water   Hot plate

Celery   Salt   Spoon (ladle)

Steps:

1. Cut up vegetables.

2. Put vegetables and soup bones into pot. Fill the pot with water and cook 1 hour.

3. Put alphabet noodles and salt into pot. Cook 10 minutes.

4. Spoon soup into bowls.

Figure 7-6
Recipe for vegetable soup.

they baked a cake to celebrate one child's birthday (they were five years old):

Planning what to put into the cake
Discussing the various ingredients
Taking turns
Grinding (wheat into flour)
Measuring
Pouring
Mixing
Stirring
Beating (with eggbeaters)
Squeezing (a lemon)
Tasting (along the way)
Smelling (the spices and the cake while it was baking)
Seeing and feeling changes (the color and consistency of the wheat as it was ground into flour)
Cleaning up (as part of the process)
Walking to the store to buy a lemon for the frosting and observing things along the way
Discussing lemon and sugar—sweet things versus sour things
Timing
Counting—how many people to be served and how many pieces to cut
Celebrating a birthday
Singing
Eating

The following types of experiences were involved:

Motor: grinding, beating, pouring, and squeezing
Sensory: tasting, smelling, touching, and seeing
Social and emotional: taking turns, having discussions, waiting, and singing
Conceptual: measuring, counting, and timing

Experimentation!

After the children have had cooking experiences and have learned to follow recipes carefully, it might be fun and interesting to provide them with some basic ingredients and some simple equipment and let them make up recipes of their own. Include items such as flour, eggs, milk, margarine, nuts, honey, brown and white sugar, and baking powder. Mixing bowls, measuring cups and measuring spoons, eggbeaters, and pans should be provided.

For the young child who is not yet writing, you can write the recipe down as the child develops it. This recipe can be saved and then referred to when the food is ready to be eaten. If the recipe does not turn out the way the child wanted it to, he or she can make some changes in it and try it again some other time.

Remember, this suggestion should be attempted only after cooking is really a strong part of the program.

Storybooks That May Promote an Interest in Cooking

AUTHOR	TITLE	PUBLISHER
Brown, M.	*Stone Soup*	Scribner
Zemach, H	*Nail Soup*	Follett
Hoban, R.	*Bread and Jam for Frances*	Faber
Kahl, Virginia	*Duchess Bakes a Cake*	Scribner
Krahn, F.	*A Flying Saucer Full of Spaghetti*	Dutton
Krauss, R.	*Carrot Seed*	Harper & Row
Oxenbury, H.	*Enormous Turnip*	Heinemann
Scheer, J.	*Rain Makes Applesauce*	Holiday
Sendak, M.	*Chicken Soup with Rice*	Collins
Sendak, M.	*In the Night Kitchen*	Harper & Row
Dr. Seuss	*Green Eggs and Ham*	Random House
Talbot, T.	*Once upon a Truffle*	Cowles

FURTHER READINGS

Baker Read, Katherine: *Ideas That Work with Young Children*, National Association for the Education of Young Children, Washington, 1972.

Croft, Karen B.: *The Good for Me Cookbook*, Science Research, Palo Alto, Calif., 1971.

Hirsch, L.: *The Block Book*, National Association for the Education of Young Children, Washington, 1974. *Kids Are Natural Cooks: Child Tested Recipes for Home and School Using Natural Foods*, Parents Nursery School, Cambridge, Mass., 1973.

Leavitte, Jerome E.: *Carpentry for Young Children*, Sterling, New York, 1971.

Moffitt, Mary W.: *Woodworking for Children*, Early Childhood Education Council of New York, New York, 1974.

GLOSSARY

ability An inborn strength, usually one that is developed with training.

acquisition The act of gaining something.

affective Having to do with emotional aspects of behavior.

attitude A position indicating feeling, opinion, or mood; a habitual reaction that reveals an opinion.

auditory discrimination The ability to distinguish differences in things that are heard.

brainstorm A sudden inspiration or idea. Brainstorming is a group process in which people spontaneously react to an idea.

capability The quality of being able to perform in some way.

capacity The ability to absorb or hold; refers to mental ability or, in mathematics, to the amount that a container will hold.

category A division that groups things on the basis of a common feature.

climate The general atmosphere.

cognitive Having to do with intellectual skills.

comprehension Understanding.

conceptualize To form a general notion or idea.

contagious Capable of being transmitted, as from one person to another, by bodily contact.

critical thinking A judgment following careful examination.

cryptogram A writing in cypher.

decode To translate from a code into the original language or form. In reading, refers to the translation of symbols into language without comprehension.

discovery learning Learning that proceeds from the known to the unknown as the result of one's own involvement.

discrimination The act of making or perceiving differences or distinctions.

early childhood Generally, the years from age three to age seven.

empathy Identification with another person's feelings, thoughts, or attitudes.

enabler One who makes something possible; one who furnishes the necessary means or power.

environment The surrounding conditions, including feelings and influences as well as objects and things.

evaluate To make a judgment concerning worth or effectiveness.

experience (*n.*) Something lived through. (*v.*) To undergo; to know by personal trial or feeling.

eye-hand coordination Coordination that results when the hand is able to follow a message given by the brain as a result of what is seen.

implement To fulfill or perform; to carry out; to put into effect according to, or by means of, a definite plan or procedure.

improvised In music, sing at the spur of the moment without preparation.

210

initiative   An introductory act or step; a leading action.

integral   Essential for completeness.

interact   To have a mutual influence or effect.

interrelated   Having a mutual connection; affecting and being affected by the same thing, feeling, or state.

manipulate   To handle, manage, or use.

motor development   The development of control over the large muscles and then the small muscles and eventually the attainment of general coordination.

mutual   Done or felt by each toward the other; given and received; shared; joint.

nonverbal   Not characterized by the use of words; communicated by means of looks, gestures, or actions.

principle   A rule or law of action or conduct; a general truth on which other truths are based.

problem solving   Finding a solution by means of trial and error; solving puzzling situations through discovery.

process   A series of motions, actions, or events; the act of going on.

progressive   Moving forward; making advancement.

reinforce   To strengthen.

sensory-motor learning   Learning about the world through the use of all five senses and through activity.

sequence   A series of things following one another characterized by a logical order of parts. In reading, sequential levels refers to the order of learning all reading skills.

seriate   (*adj.*) Arranged or occurring in a series; (*v.*) To put in order according to size, color, or shape, for example.

skill   An ability or mastered technique.

symbol   Something that stands for or represents something else.

transition   The time between activities or blocks of time.

verbal behavior   What a person says.

visual discrimination   The ability to distinguish differences in things that are seen.

visual memory   The ability to reproduce and recall accurately something that was seen before.

APPENDIX

SOURCES OF INFORMATION

Association for Childhood Educational International
3615 Wisconsin Avenue N.W.
Washington, D.C. 20016

Bank Street College of Education
Publications Department
Day Care Consultation Service and Center for Day Care Training
610 West 112th Street
New York, New York 10025

Black Child Development Institute
Suite 514 1028 Connecticut Avenue N.W.
Washington, D.C. 20036

Bureau of Child Development and Parent Education
Albany, New York 12201

Canadian Welfare Council Research Branch
55 Pardale Avenue
Ottawa, 3, Ontario

Children's Foundation
1026 Seventeenth Street N.W.
Washington, D.C. 20036
  (Information on Special Food Service
  Program of National School Lunch Act)

Child Study Association of America
9 East 89 Street
New York, New York 10028

Child Welfare League of America
44 East 23d Street
New York, New York 10010

Day Care and Child Development Council of America
1401 K Street N.W.
Washington, D.C. 20005

Educational Development Center
55 Chapel Street
Cambridge, Massachusetts 02138

Educational Facilities Laboratories
477 Madison Avenue
New York, New York 10032

Educational Resources Information Center (ERIC)
U.S. Department of Health, Education, and Welfare
Office of Education
Washington, D.C. 20202

Interstate Research Association
3210 Grace Street N.W.
Washington, D.C. 20009
  (Bilingual bicultural child care)

National Association for the Education of Young Children
1834 Connecticut Avenue N.W.
Washington, D.C. 20009

National Parents Federation for Day Care and Child Development
429 Lewis Street
Somerset, New Jersey 08873

National Welfare Rights Organization
1424 Sixteenth Street N.W.
Washington, D.C. 20036

New England Free Press
791 Tremont Street
Boston, Massachusetts 02118

N.O.W. (National Organization for Women)
Task Force on Child Care
45 Newburry Street
Boston, Massachusetts 02116

Women's Action Alliance
Room 313 370 Lexington Avenue
New York, New York 10017

Government Agencies

Child Nutrition Division
U.S. Department of Agriculture
Washington, D.C. 20250

Office of Child Development
U.S. Department of Health, Education, and Welfare
400 Sixth Street S.W.
Washington, D.C. 20201

Office of Economic Opportunity
1200 Ninth Street N.W.
Washington, D.C. 20036

Social and Rehabilitation Service
Community Services Administration
330 C Street S.W.
Washington, D.C. 20201
  (Title IVA Funding)

Women's Bureau
U.S. Department of Labor
Washington, D.C. 20210

Free Catalogues to Help You Review Equipment and Materials

Looking at other child-care centers is the best way to learn what children do and what materials they use. But catalogues are helpful. They can also give you ideas for things to make or buy. Sometimes the same equipment is available at the local five-and-ten or stationery store at a lower price.

These major suppliers will send you free catalogues. Tell them that you represent a child-care center and give the ages of the children in your program.

Childcraft Education Corp.
964 Third Avenue
New York, New York 10002

Child Life
Highland Street
Holliston, Massachusetts 01746

Community Playthings
Department 2
Rifton, New York 12471

Creative Playthings
Princeton, New Jersey

J. L. Hammett Co.
Hammett Place
Braintree, Massachusetts 02184

Judy Materials
General Learning Corp.

Early Learning Division
310 N. Second Street
Minneapolis, Minnesota 55401

Macmillan Co.
Early Childhood Discovery Materials
866 Third Avenue
New York, New York 10022

NOVO Educational Toys Corp.
585 Avenue of the Americas
New York, New York 10001

Selective Education Equipment
3 Bridge Street
Newton, Massachusetts 02158

Teaching Aids
A Division of A. Daigg and Co.
159 West Kinzie Street
Chicago, Illinois 60610

Xerox Corp.
P.O. Box 381
Beacon, New York 12508

Materials and Equipment for the Children's Center

The following booklets on building equipment are available from Early
Childhood Education Study, Advisory on Open Education, 90 Sherman
Street, Cambridge, Massachusetts: 02160

Building with Cardboard. A booklet showing how to work with cardboard. Includes instructions and designs for tables, bookcases, stolls,
easels, playhouses, and puppet stages. Charge.

Building with Tubes. A booklet showing how to work with heavy
cardboard tubes, which are normally discarded by business and indus-
try, to make stools, tables, cubbies, shelves, etc. Charge.

Cardboard Carpentry Introduction. A thirty-eight page picture book
giving ideas for kinds of equipment that can be built from triple-strength
cardboard. Charge.

Other helpful publications include:

Musical Instruments Recipe Book and *Whistles and Strings.* Published by Elementary Science Study, 55 Chapel Street, Newton, Massachusetts 02158. Charge.

From the Ground Up: A Book of Ideas for Pre-School Equipment. Send request to CDGM Vincent Building, 203 West Capital Street, Jackson, Mississippi. Everything in this book was designed and made by people in the local community for their community-run center.

Matterson, E. C.: *Play and Playthings for the Pre-School Child.* Penguin, Baltimore, 1967. Charge. An informative text on activities involving sand, water, clay, wood, and musical instruments. Contains lists of children's books and also has diagrams showing how to build equipment.

Pre-School Equipment: For a Multi-Use Center. Prepared by Stone Mountain Education Projects, Inc., Roaring Brook Farm, Conway, Massachusetts 01341. Send request to Stone Mountain, 50 Broad Street, Westfield, Massachusetts 01085. Charge. Gives ideas for equipment which is portable and inexpensive to make, and which provides its own storage. Useful for programs that share space with other groups and have to store or move their equipment at the end of each day or week.

Periodicals of Interest

There are numerous magazines and journals devoted to child care and early childhood education. Some that may interest you are:

Childhood Education. Published by the Association for Childhood Education International. Membership in the organization includes the magazine.

Children Today. Issued six times a year by the U.S. Department of Health, Education, and Welfare, Children's Bureau. Subscription charge.

Day Care and Early Education. Published by Behavioral Publications, 72 Fifth Avenue, New York, New York 10011, five times a year; $9.75

Interracial Books for Children. Published eight times a year by Council on Interracial Books for Children, 1841 Broadway, New York, N.Y. 10023; individual subscription $8 a year.

Voice for Children. Newsletter of the Day Care and Child Development Council of America. Included in membership in the organization.

Young Children. Issued six times a year by the National Association for Education of Young Children. Members of the association receive the magazine as part of the membership; nonmembers can subscribe for a charge.

Bibliographies of Children's Books

The following are sources for books dealing with children from different ethnic and racial groups and with men and women taking nonstereotypical roles:

Black Experience in Children's Books. New York Public Library, Office of Children's Services, 8 East 40th Street, New York, New York 10016. Charge.

China Books and Periodicals, 2929 24th Street, San Francisco, California, or 125 Fifth Avenue, New York, New York.

Circle Associates, Afro-American Studies Resources Center, 126 Warren Avenue, Roxbury, Massachusetts. This organization provides lists of children's books which emphasize ethnic and racial diversity.
Feminist Press, Box 334, Old Westbury, New York 11568.

Little Ms. Muffet Fights Back. Published by Feminists of Children's Media, P.O. Box 4315, Grand Central Station, New York, New York 10010. Charge plus a 4- by 9-inch self-addressed, stamped envelope. Send request to Lillipop Power, P.O. Box 1171, Chapel Hill, North Carolina 27514.

Ms., 370 Lexington Avenue, New York, New York. The Spring 1972 issue contains a bibliography (pp. 30–32), or you can send directly to the *Ms.* office for a more complete list.

INDEX

Activities:
  auditory discrimination, 103
  classifying, 104
  matching, sorting, and grouping,
    82–85
  math, 104–127
  pre-reading, 102–104
  visual discrimination, 104
Adjustment to school, 43–48
Advisor, college, 6
  (*See also* Supervisor, college)
Allergies, 167
Anecdotal record, 36–38
Art, 94, 152–164
  in blocks, 182
  the creative process, 152–159
  display of children's work, 70
  do's and don'ts, 159–161
  in housekeeping area, 95
  materials, 161–163
  in outdoor play, 172
  recipes, 163–164
  room arrangement, 64–65, 69,
    72–73
  science learning in, 132
  in woodworking, 189
Attitudes with children, 6–7

Auditory discrimination, 90–91
  activities for, 103
  in music, 147
  in pre-reading, 99

Blocks, 180–183
  as learning experience, 61–62
  math learning in, 62
  observing use of, 40
  room arrangement, 61–64, 72
  science learning, 132
  social studies, 142
  storage, 62–63
  teacher's role, 91–92, 182–183
Books in library area, 66–67, 73
  (*See also* Library; Reading stories)

Case study, 38
Check list, 38
Classifying, 104
  (*See also* Learning; Matching;
    Sorting)
Classroom personnel, 13
  (*See also* Teaching profession)

222

Cognitive development:
activities for, 80–81
importance of language in, 81–82
value of play in, 88–92
(*See also* Intellectual development)
Communicable diseases, 168–169
Community:
children's, 10
in social studies, 140–141
(*See also* Culture; Parents)
Comparing, matching and, 79
Comprehension skills, 107–109
critical reading, 109
interpretive comprehension, 108
literal comprehension, 108
Configuration clues, 105–106
Conjunctivitis, 167
Context clues, 105, 106
Cooking, 194–208
helpful hints, 196
recipes, 196–206
stories that include, 208
value of, 194–195, 205–207
Creative process in art, 152–159
Critical reading, 109
Culture:
cultural conditions, 3–4
and food, 165
and music, 152
(*See also* Community; Parents)
Curriculum (*see* Integrated curriculum)
Curriculum goals, 42–43

Directionality, 100
Discipline, 50–57
do's and don'ts, 56
in room arrangement, 70–71
setting limits, 53
Dramatic play, 85–89
in housekeeping area, 86
in social studies, 142
(*See also* Dress-up clothes)
Dress-up clothes, 61, 71, 74

Emotional development, 22–28
in blocks, 181
in music, 146
observing, 39
Epilepsy, 168
Equipment:
art, 161–163

Equipment:
in cooking, 196–205
outdoor, 175–176
in science area, 133
woodworking, 191–192
(*See also* Room arrangement)

Family (*see* Culture; Community; Parents)
Finger plays, math learning, 124–129
First aid, 167–168
bleeding, 167
cuts, 167
nosebleeds, 168
Freud, Anna, 44

Games (*see* Activities)
Grouping:
activities for, 83–85
sorting and, 79–80
Growth and development, 20–31
for three- to five-year old, 25–31
uneven, 25

Health education, 94, 164–176
food, 165
in housekeeping area, 96
in integrated curriculum, 96
outdoor play, 169–175
(*See also* Physical education)
Housekeeping area:
and curriculum areas, 95–96
in dramatic play, 86
in room arrangement, 61, 69, 71–72, 74
and science learning, 132
in social studies, 142
Humor in storytelling, 114

Impetigo, 166
Individual differences, 9–10, 20, 25
in adjustment to school, 43–44
Integrated curriculum, 94–97, 180–208
and art, 96
and blocks, 180–183
and cooking, 194–208
and health education, 96
and langauge arts, 95–96
and math, 95–96, 118

Integrated curriculum:
  and music, 95–96
  and science, 95–96
  and social studies, 95–96
  and trips, 183–188
  and woodworking, 188–194
  (*See also* Curriculum)
Intellectual development, 22–24,
    29–31
  in blocks, 182
  in music, 146
  observing, 40
  stages of, 31–33
  (*See also* Cognitive development;
      Learning; Piaget, Jean)
Interpretive comprehension, 108–
    109

Kluckhorn, Clyde, 20

Language, recording children's, 40
  (*See also* Langauge arts)
Language arts, 94, 97–117
  in blocks, 182
  in housekeeping area, 95
  in integrated curriculum, 95–96
  and learning process, 81
  pre-reading, 99–104
  reading skills, 104–113
  reading stories, 113–117
  the teacher and, 97
  and trips, 186
  and woodworking, 188–189
Learning:
  with blocks, 180
  children's, 78
  through dramatic play, 85
  implications for classroom, 80–81
  in language development, 81–82
  matching and comparing, 79
  process of, 20–22, 78
  sorting and grouping, 79–80
  about things, 78
  and trust, 92
  using the senses, 78
  value of play in, 88–91
Left to right orientation, 100
Library in room arrangement, 66,
    69, 73
Lice, 167
Listening (*see* Auditory discrimina-
    tion)
Literal comprehension, 108

Manipulative toys in room arrange-
    ment, 64, 72
Matching:
  activities for, 82–83
  and comparing, 79
Mathematics, 94, 96, 117–129
  in blocks, 182
  and everyday experiences, 119
  and everyday materials, 118–119
  finger plays, 128–129
  games, 124–129
  geometry, 122
  in housekeeping area, 95
  in integrated curriculum, 118
  measurement, 121–122
  number skills, 120–121
  personal, 122–123
  vocabulary, 123–124
  in woodworking, 188
Motor coordination in pre-reading,
    100
  (*See also* Sensory motor develop-
      ment)
Movement, 150
Music, 94, 96, 145–152
  in block area, 182
  and listening, 147
  and movement, 150
  and outdoor play, 171–172
  in room arrangement, 66, 69
  science learning in, 132
  and singing, 147–148
  teacher's role in, 146–147
  in trips, 186
  using musical instruments, 149–
    150
  in woodworking, 189
Musical instruments, 149–150

Observing, 34–40
  nonverbal behavior, 34–36
  questions for, 37–38
  suggestions for, 39–40
  and using records, 36–38
  the whole child, 34–40
Outdoor play, 169–176
  basic equipment, 175–176
  and science, 133

Paraprofessional, 3
Parents:
  and curriculum aims, 43
  and nutrition, 165

224 Parents:
  and outdoor play, 170
  as primary relationship, 44
  role in music, 152
  role during school adjustment,
      44–48
  role in social studies, 141
  role on trips, 184–186
  in school, 48–50
  and separation, 44–48
  the student teacher and, 13
  (*See also* Community)
Phonics, 105–107
Physical development, 22–26
  in blocks, 180
  in music, 145
  observing, 39
Physical education in woodworking,
      189
  (*See also* Health education)
Physical symptoms, 165–167
  in conjunctivitis, 167
  in impetigo, 166
  of lice, 167
  related to ears, 165
  related to eyes, 165
  related to urination, 166
  in ringworm, 166
Piaget, Jean, 31–33
Pictures clues, 105–106
Play:
  teacher's role in, 91–92
  value of, 88–92
  (*See also* Dramatic play)
Pre-operational stage, 32
Pre-reading, 99–104
  activities and games for, 102–104

Reading readiness (*see* Pre-reading)
Reading skills, 104–113
  comprehension, 107–109
  reading games, 112–113
  reading systems and, 110–112
  study skills, 109–110
  word recognition, 104–107
Reading stories, 113–117
Reading systems, 110–112
Recipes, cooking (*see* Cooking)
Recording, 36–37
Rogers, Carl, 159*n.*
Ringworm, 166
Room arrangement, 60–76
  and color, 70
  condition of equipment in ,69

Room arrangement:
  effect on children's behavior, 60
  evaluation, 70–74
  kit for, 74–76
  relationship between interest
      areas, 67
  picture displays, 70
  placement of interest areas, 69
  size of areas, 69
  storage of materials, 69
  traffic patterns, 69
  variety of materials, 69

Sand:
  room arrangement, 66
  science learning, 133–134
Science, 94, 130–138
  areas of study, 134
  in blocks, 182
  in housekeeping area, 95, 132
  in integrated curriculum, 95–96
  outdoor play and, 170–173
  scientific attitudes, 135
  scientific concepts, 134–135
  scientific method, 134–137
  teachers' role in, 137–138
  and woodworking, 188
Self-control, 50, 56
  (*See also* Discipline)
Self-image:
  helped in room arrangement, 74
  in music, 151
Senses, use of, 78, 88
  (*See also* Sensorimotor develop-
      ment)
Sensorimotor development:
  motor coordination, 127–128
  in Piaget's work, 31–32
  (*See also* Senses)
Separation and trips, 187
  (*See also* Adjustment to school)
Sex roles (*see* Social roles)
Singing, 147–148
Small group games (*see* Manipula-
      tive toys)
Snack, 81
  and discipline, 50–51
  health education, 165
  outdoors, 170
  and science learning, 133
Social development, 22–24, 28
  and blocks, 180
  observing, 39

Social development:
  in music, 146
Social roles:
  in block area, 72
  and dress-up clothes, 71, 87
  in housekeeping area, 61
  and self-image, 74
  women's role in woodworking, 194
Social studies, 94, 138–144
  and blocks, 142, 182
  and dramatic play, 142
  in integrated curriculum, 95–96
  unifying curriculum, 143–144
  woodworking, 188
Sorting:
  activities for, 83–85
  and grouping, 79–80
Story telling, 113–117
  outdoors, 170–171
Structural analysis, 105, 107
Student teacher, 4–6, 13–17
  evaluation of, 16
  and parents, 13
  self-awareness of, 2–4
  (*See also* Teaching profession)
Study skills, 109–110
Supervisor:
  college, 15–17
    (*See also* Advisor)
  school, 11

Table toys (*see* Manipulative toys)
Teacher's role, 7–11
  in art, 154–161
  in blocks, 182–183
  in child's adjustment to school,
    44–46
  in discipline, 51–57
  in language arts, 97–98
  in music, 146–147
  in outdoor play, 173–175
  in play, 91–92

Teacher's role:
  in science, 137–138
  in social studies, 140–142
  on trips, 184–187
Teaching profession:
  attitude towards, 2–4
  choice of, 2–4
  school personnel, 11–13
  (*See also* Student teacher)
Thinking, children's, 31–33
  (*See also* Cognitive development;
      Intellectual development;
      Piaget, Jean)
Trips, 183–188
  ideas for, 187–188
Trust and learning, 92

Visual discrimination, 89
  activities for, 104
  in pre-reading, 99
Visual memory, 100

Water play:
  math, 119
  outdoors, 171
  room arrangement, 66, 69
Whole child, 22–31
  curriculum aims, 42–43
  observing and recording, 34–40
  programs for, 25–31
  understanding of, 25–31
Woodworking, 188–194
  helpful hints, 192–194
  materials, 191
  math learning in, 118
  outdoors, 170
  room arrangement, 66, 69, 73
  science learning, 132
  women's role and, 194
Word recognition skills, 104–107